Negotiation
Your Hottest Currency

Jan Potgieter

Negotiation
Your Hottest Currency

Jan Potgieter

Contents

Foreword

When you build a billion-dollar company, there are specific days that leave a permanent impression.

In the development of TomTom as a global technology company, my team and I got to experience the highs and lows that are common to all entrepreneurs, but magnified a million times.

I will never forget the day I received the report that we had sold one million units of our portable navigation device - the TomTom Go - in one calendar year. It felt like an enormous triumph for a group of four young people who started with a dream to make the roads a little safer.

Then there was the day we learned that we had sold one million units in just one calendar month. Followed shortly by the report that we had sold one million units in one week. At last, there came the day we sold one million units in a single day. Heady stuff.

We were riding the ultimate wave of success, far from the sobering day in 2004, when we rolled out the TomTom Navigator to looks of shock and contempt at a trade show. They said we couldn't do it. We were a software company; hardware was outside our wheelhouse. They said GPS systems would be built into cars. Frankly, they said we were out of our minds. Maybe we didn't communicate our vision effectively; maybe they weren't ready to receive it. Either way, our message fell flat at first. Investors were equally skeptical; they couldn't see the future we could see.

But then the market saw it. They embraced our devices and bought them by the millions. Orders flooded in. The press came calling.

We disrupted a whole industry in a short window of time. We went from having to explain what we were doing at dinner parties to being feted as celebrities in public. We saturated the market, which sounds good until you realize that there comes a point where everyone has one and doesn't need another. The demand goes down, the price goes down, the sparkle begins to fade. We began to see warning signs that uncertain times were ahead.

In the midst of that rush there is another day that sticks out in our collective memories. It's the day that Google released its proprietary GPS navigation services, for free, across all platforms, including smartphones. In 2008, smartphones weren't nearly as smart as they are today, but Google had kicked the door open and we knew that, if we wanted to survive this cataclysmic disruption to our world, we needed to pivot quickly and definitively.

2008 was also the year the economy of the entire planet came screeching to a halt. Europe took it especially hard. That kind of thing is never good for business, but we knew we were smart business people and we figured we could ride it out. However, we were also a couple of billion Euros in debt because we had just completed the purchase of digital mapping company, TeleAtlas. The deal made perfect sense when we were the market leader in a good economy, but didn't look nearly as practical to outsiders when the market gave way.

It would have been easy to run to the hills and hide, but that is not who we are.

In the years that followed, we came back stronger and better-equipped to weather difficult times. Resilience is key to survival in any endeavor, but especially when all seems lost. We diversified our business and re-examined our alliances. And we accepted that there were opportunities from which we simply needed to walk away.

Perhaps more importantly, I recognized that I had a responsibility to take what I had learned and invest it into others.

I knew that I had attained a place in the business world that few people—and even fewer women—ever reach. I was leading a multi-billion-dollar global company and before this, I had travelled the world, making an impact. For Psion, I had brought laptops and touch pads to places like Russia, Turkey, and Israel. In1990, I had used these same devices to facilitate the first democratic election of government officials in post-Soviet Hungary. But I also had a responsibility to mentor other women to climb to the heights of their full potential, and to do something significant from their positions of influence.

I also recognized that we needed a new generation of digitally literate people to shape the future. Machine and information technologies are quietly influencing every aspect of our lives, from our workplace to our automobiles to our refrigerators, and our success in life is tied directly to our ability to harness and control that technology. It is a skill I saw entirely lacking from our government-run school systems (and even from most private schools). We have allowed ourselves to be victims of technology; we must learn to control it. There simply are not enough programmers in the world. Fortunately, we are seeing real change in this area.

I am thinking now of another transformative date in my life—the one of which I am perhaps the most proud. I built CODAM, a technology school in Amsterdam to train and equip a generation of programmers to shape the future of technology. It's free, open to all, and uses peer-to-peer learning. No-one was certain that such a school was feasible, but we took a measured risk—and it has paid off. Enrollment is quickly approaching 1,000 students, and a good percentage are young women who are waking up to the realization that they can make a real difference in the world. Building CODAM has truly been the most rewarding thing I could have hoped to do with my life, aside from raising two wise and intelligent sons and cultivating a strong marriage with a brilliant husband.

I have often said that the ability to program computers is the single most important key to success in the future. But if I had to pick a second skill with equivalent power to transform the world, it is the ability to negotiate effectively. That is why I am so delighted that you have this book in your hands.

I want to leave you with the memory of one more significant day from my career. It was at a negotiation training seminar led by your author, Jan Potgieter. I experienced what I could only describe as a "revelation."

As Jan was walking us through a real-world simulation that applied the principles of best and leading practice business negotiation, I recognized that so much of the success in deal making can be attributed to my ability to apply these principles to all of my interactions—not only at TomTom, but at home, at speaking engagements… everywhere. Had I left unrealized value on the table? Had I missed opportunities to wield influence with people? Perhaps.

Mind you, I had been to business school. I had overseen an international sales organization. I had been running a global company for years. If anyone could be described as an accomplished negotiator, it was me. You would think I would have known all the techniques and strategies outlined in this book like the road to my house. Yet I was exposed to insights that I still use every day.

What Jan showed me that day—which was just a portion of the contents of this book—opened my eyes to aspects of dealing with humans that I had never seen before. It was transformative for me, and I believe it will be for you, as well.

My wish for you is that you would have a similar enlightening as you study this book. I adjure you: do not just gloss over it as another business book, but absorb the contents as the roadmap to your future business success.

I do not overstate the matter to say that your success—in business, in your community, and in your relationships—is on the other side of these principles.

Imagine sitting across from a stone-faced purchasing agent, an aggressive competitor, or even a belligerent teenager, and quietly winning them over to your way of thinking—without coercion, manipulation, or raising your voice. Imagine forming a multi-million-dollar strategic partnership with a company you thought was unapproachable. Imagine taking your partner on the vacation you wanted to take, instead of always acquiescing to their preferences. The skills taught in this book will facilitate changes like those.

Jan is a world-class teacher and coach, and I count on him to advance my top employees to their best performance, His experience across more than 20 years and 60 nations is as broad and diverse as that of anyone else I have known, and his unique perspective challenges me to think at a different level.

I am delighted to introduce this book to you and I look forward to someday reading about how you used these principles to make your unique mark on the world.

Corinne Vigreux
Co-Founder
TomTom

Acknowledgements

Writing a book is an undertaking that relies on contributions from many people in addition to the author. I'd like to thank the following people for making this book possible:

Linda Potgieter, my partner in business and life, for helping me to turn twenty years' worth of teaching, experience and stories into a guide that can help anyone to negotiate like a professional.

Professor Manie Spoelstra for introducing me to the body of knowledge that supports the art & science of negotiation.

Dr. David Venter for sharing his vast experience with me and challenging my thinking around the implementation of negotiation best and leading practices.

Chad Ketcher for providing editorial and project management support.

The thousands of business professionals that have gone through our training over the past seventeen years.

The companies and individual that have engaged our consulting services serving as the proving ground for the strategies, tactics, techniques and tools that are to be found in this book.

Dedication

This book is dedicated to my wife, Linda Potgieter. Linda is the most teachable person I know and her desire for constant improvement in all areas of life has fueled my own personal and professional development to make me capable far beyond my own level of skill. Thank you for encouraging me, bringing out the best in me and for gracefully dealing with my frequent absences from home and family as I traveled the world delivering training and consultancy projects.

Introduction

Who is the most ruthless, cutthroat business type character you can think of?

While you picture that person in your mind, I'll tell you about my older brother, Reenen Potgieter. Reenen is an attorney in South Africa, specializing in commercial litigation.

He is as ruthless and fearless a lawyer as you would expect to see in the movies, played by Robert DeNiro or Javier Bardem. He's that guy that puts people in the witness stand and circles them until they slip up. His game is to pull them apart on behalf of his clients.

I recently asked him, "How do you win a case in law?"

"Number one," he intoned without a hint of emotion, "you win because you are correct on the point of law. Number two, you win because you tear the witness apart." Just like you have two or three favorite clubs in your golf bag, he has favorite tools and techniques he uses to make witnesses implode on themselves.

"What about the relationship?" I asked, "You win the argument, but what happens to the relationship?"

Without missing a beat, he responded coolly, "By the time it gets to my desk, we are long beyond caring about the relationship."

Breaking Down False Stereotypes

Why would I start a book about professional negotiation skills with a reference to a cutthroat business character?

Because everywhere I've been (on six continents), I meet people—from first-time entrepreneurs to Fortune-100 CEOs—who believe in their hearts that this is what negotiation is: ruthless men in silk suits going head-to-head like cage fighters, trying to break each other down over a dispute.

Now, having introduced you to my brother's professional persona for the purpose of illustration, I owe it to him to state for the record that he is one of my favorite people in the world. He is a man of high integrity and ethics, a loving family man, and a good friend who enjoys fine wine and a good joke.

It's Time To Clear The Air

I wrote this book to empower people in the world of business (which, for our purposes, includes for-profit, non-profit, and government organizations) with the skills and tools to deal with important, high value, complex and/or cross-cultural commercial negotiations. My motivation as a negotiation trainer has always been to remove the mystery behind the art and science of successful negotiation.

For too long, the subject of negotiation has been either clouded in an academic shroud or presented in such a tactical "street fighting" sense that it has little use in complex and high-value negotiations. In this book, I will challenge many of the traditional beliefs and approaches to negotiation emanating from the establishment (large, well-known universities in the USA and Europe) and conventional negotiation skills training providers.

For instance, we will directly call into question the benefits of linear and sequential approaches to negotiation and challenge you to deliver negotiation results that are not only based on trust and integrity, but also mutually beneficial and sustainable. My desire is that this book will help you and your organization rise to a world-class capability in deal-making.

To do that, we need to go back to the fundamentals and quickly get our terminology on the same page.

What Is Negotiation?

I'm always amused by the misconceptions people have about negotiation.

Most people understand negotiation to be something international diplomats or sales managers do; a chess match between rivals that one will win and one will lose. They might think of it as an isolated step in the process of sales or purchasing, and when it does happen, it's seen as an event—infrequent at best— rather than an ongoing process.

The truth is very different, and my hope is that by shedding light on the real meaning, purpose and value of negotiation, you will see how it can integrate into every part of your life.

The Latin root of the word negotiation, *negotiatus*, literally means "to carry on business." From that basis, you can see that negotiation encompasses every part of your business interactions, including sales, management, purchasing, and even human resources.

You can also apply it more broadly to all of your interactions in any arena of life. To the extent that negotiation involves persuasion and influence, isn't there an element of negotiation that takes place in your home—with your spouse, children, and neighbors? That is why I am so excited about how this book can reach beyond the corporate boardroom and impact you on a personal level.

But more on that later.

For now, let's establish a working definition of negotiation where both the art and science of negotiation are nothing more and nothing less than communication in a business-specific context. It is not the preserve of presidents and professors; it is not limited to the formal exchanges that happen when you discuss the contractual terms of a deal. Simply put, negotiation occurs whenever you're doing business, and it includes the interactions you have with those who work alongside or in support of you.

Missing Out On The Bigger Picture

As the conventional understanding of negotiation is becoming more narrow and marginalized, we see organizations of all sizes relegating negotiation to a role on the sales team. Some groups have split their resources into teams that focus on buying or selling on behalf of the organization. The notion that any act of doing business—or indeed anything that is not leisure—is a form of negotiation has been clouded over by our need to make sense of the highly complex nature of the large organizations that are so typical of the modern world.

Even seasoned leaders and executives fall into the trap of thinking that negotiation is something that only takes place when it comes to the time to agree on a price or sign a contract. The opportunities missed to both create and claim value through negotiation in the larger sense are profound.

I've made this same mistake in the past, and I'd be willing to bet you have, too. Because you've been so busy chasing your targets and objectives, you may not have invested adequately in preparing for negotiations and, as a result, have probably made two key mistakes:

Maintaining An Event Mindset: You've been focused on the upcoming negotiation as an event. In other words, you've been thinking about how you will present your case during the formal meetings that you know are coming once you've been selected as the successful vendor. On the other hand, maybe you're a buyer and you've been focused on how you will twist your selected vendor's arm to lower their price.

Failure To Measure Negotiation Success: You have not been measuring your own performance and/or your team's success at negotiating. How will you be able to improve the way that you negotiate if you have no idea how you stack up against best and leading practices? As famously stated by American engineer and management consultant, W. Edwards Deming, "You can't manage what you don't measure."

Let's do a quick self-assessment:

- Are you a better negotiator now than you were five years, ten years, or fifteen years ago?

- Have you changed the way you approach negotiations or are you just approaching negotiation by default?

- Have you cultivated many years of diversified negotiation experience or have you just picked up some negotiation habits that have stuck?

The more honest you are with yourself about questions like these and others I will present in this book, the faster you can achieve world class results as a negotiator.

What Is A Professional Negotiator?

At this point, you might be tempted to put down the book and say, "I have no intention of being a professional negotiator, so I guess I'm done here." Actually, you're the person I'm most interested in speaking to, because there are strategies, tactics, and techniques in this book that people who don't think of themselves as professional negotiators can use every day to dramatically change their circumstances for the better. If you promise to keep reading, I promise to give you simple and effective tools to enhance all of your business opportunities and relationships.

You will find tools in this book that will help you bring greater value to your workplace, increase your influence in your community, restore harmony (and even romance) to your marriage, and become a hero to your children. How do I know? Because I take these skills home with me every day. And they have significantly impacted the quality of my relationships at home.

The best part is that these strategies, tactics, and techniques are honest, ethical, integrous, and relationship driven. I will not teach you to shred people. Instead, I will show you how to build bridges to better relationships, more money, more fun, and more positive impact.

So, when I talk about achieving elite-level negotiation results, I'm not only talking to Fortune-500 executives but also to independent contractors, small business owners, coaches, moms, husbands, school administrators, PTA members, and neighbors.

With that in mind, let me ask you the next important question to help frame your journey: Do you think of yourself as a professional negotiator?

Your answer to this question will go a long way to shaping both your expectations and results.

Understanding the Word

My definition of a professional negotiator (according to the Latin root of the word) is "anyone who is in any way involved in doing business—or for that matter, anything outside of their leisure time." Does that cover what you do?

The professional negotiation community is made up of those who negotiate to do business, plain and simple. Transactions are negotiated between people and between organizations daily. Agreements are negotiated within organizations internally by the hour, during every meeting, and even in every conversation, email and phone call that takes place between colleagues and business partners. Wherever these two activities take place you will find professional business negotiators in action.

Although you may not consider yourself to be a professional negotiator, the fact is that you should be one. Most of those in the business world don't even realize they are negotiating all day, every day.

How does that understanding change the game for you? If you were consciously aware that almost every interaction with your colleagues and counterparts represented a negotiation opportunity, would you be convinced to apply negotiation best practices to ensure that you get the best possible results?

Are you starting to see the opportunity for competitive differentiation?

It's Not What You Might Be Thinking

Now, I'm not suggesting that you'll become a "professional negotiator" in the sense that you'll be called upon to facilitate peace treaties between warring nations. As a matter of fact, it has always been interesting to me to see how people respond when we meet for the first time outside of a work setting. When I explain that I am a professional negotiation trainer and consultant, people often think that it means I have something to do with the United Nations, hostage scenarios, or international dispute resolution. Very few people make the connection that we negotiate daily in our business environments.

As such, the opportunity that awaits the professional negotiator is profound.

One thing that surprises me about the negotiation training industry is that so many negotiation trainers advocate the idea that almost all negotiations are similar, and that the point of departure is the assumption that there is some kind of conflict present between the respective positions assumed by the parties to the negotiation.

This is a fear-based mindset.

What you focus on in life is what you'll get more of, and if your basic assumption is that negotiation is centered on resolving conflict (rather than the act of simply doing business) then I suspect that you will find your life is full of conflict.

Suggesting that all negotiations are the same is like saying that all sports are the same. Following that logic, a great competitive sailor is also a great marathon runner. While you certainly will share many characteristics with other athletes—eating healthy, thinking competitively, displaying a high degree of training discipline—your particular code of sport will require you to master vastly different techniques and tactics than other athletes in order for you to be successful.

It is no different in the world of doing business. As a successful and professional business negotiator, you will share many of the characteristics of successful negotiators in areas like conflict resolution or hostage negotiations, but you will also be the master of many business-specific negotiation strategies, tactics, and techniques.

Let me be specific: this book is not about creating great generalist negotiators. It is not about telling you about how to be a mediator, hostage negotiator or conflict and dispute resolution expert (even though the strategies we'll cover will probably equip you to do well in any of those areas). I've written this book specifically with the modern businessperson in mind.

All Change, No Change?

If you have been in the business world for any length of time, you have likely observed that our collective culture has completely transformed from what was the norm as little as fifty years ago:

- We work more on our own and less in task-driven, collegial, industrial settings.

- We obtain and consume food in ways that might have confused our parents and grandparents.

- Our populations are congregating in urban centers more than at any time in history.

- We spend our leisure time in ways that would have been unfamiliar to previous generations.

- We structure organizations and governments more democratically than ever before

- We interact with others using communication platforms almost unrecognizable from the way the world operated even as recently as 2000.

By contrast, the way that negotiation skills development has been taught has largely remained unchanged. So much has changed in how we communicate (using email, phones, social media and video conferencing in addition to face to face meetings) and with whom we communicate (people from all over the world rather than only people from our own cultural background), that it has rendered obsolete much of what has been traditionally taught in the negotiation skills development classroom.

So much of what was advocated as negotiation best practice was (and still is) founded on a flawed, linear assumption that largely discounts human nature and revolves around a mono-cultural mode of interaction rooted in a North American, British, or European perspective.

You see, while the world is changing around us, due to the runaway train of globalization, anthropologists and psychologists largely agree that human nature itself has not changed much over thousands of years.

Against this backdrop, I find it astonishing that so much of what continues to be taught by many so-called "negotiation experts" has its roots in:

- research conducted mainly among groups of undergraduate students

- the specific context of conflict resolution scenarios (e.g., labor relations, peace treaties, big corporate disasters, etc.)

Let me also be clear on this point: while there is useful learning to be gleaned from the research studies done by the academic institutions, the premise for that research is too narrow and, to a large extent, discounts the lowest common denominator that ties people together. This research has largely ignored human nature and has narrowed the focus of what is deemed to be "negotiation" to such a niche definition that it mostly revolves around finding ways to reach agreement around a set of so-called "conflicting interests."

So Much More Than Conflict Resolution

Now, don't get me wrong, there often will be a conflict of interests present between parties to a negotiation. But to start with the assumption that negotiation is only a means of conflict resolution or closing formal transactions is to completely ignore the original roots of the word (***negotiatus***: to do business) and creates an expectation that does not best serve the objective of reaching lasting and mutually beneficial agreements.

I like how Merriam Webster's Dictionary defines the term, human nature: "The ways of thinking, feeling, and acting that are common to most people and the nature of humans; especially: the fundamental dispositions and traits of humans."

Let's start with that as a basis for our discussion.

If we can agree that human nature is common to all humans and that (for the moment, at least) we negotiate with humans, then why would we choose to put the focus of negotiation on finding solutions to conflicting interests, when the reality is that, at a root level, we all share the same set of interests?

Wouldn't it make more sense to tap into that which is shared and common amongst all people and peoples—irrespective of gender, culture, or age—to move toward reaching an agreement?

A Novel Approach

In this book, I will approach negotiation from a novel perspective: that human nature ties us all together with the same fundamental dispositions and desires. I will put forward the case that to get the most from your negotiations you have to both understand human nature and then harness it to deliver the results you are seeking from your negotiations.

There are certainly parts of the conventional academic research which overlap with this study of human nature, and I will point to some of those studies in support of the contents that will follow. If you can understand the opportunities offered by human nature for optimizing your negotiation results, you will be able to apply fantastically powerful negotiation strategies, techniques, and tactics across cultures (the last time I checked all cultures were made up of humans), over all forms of communication, and across gender and generation gaps. You will be surprised at how easily you will be able to move your own approach to negotiation from one of default to one of design.

Approaching negotiation by design rather than by default will forever change the results you will achieve from your interactions with others. A simple fact of life is that your results in business and in relationships are a direct reflection of your ability to negotiate and connect with people.

Why do I say this?

How Top People Get To The Top

When you look at large organizations, the key skill that people at the top of those organizations have mastered is the skill of relating to others in a way that allows them to achieve their own objectives within a vocational context (even if many of them lack the skill to transfer this to a family setting).

It's simply not possible to get to the top of large organizations without the support of others. This is how I know they've mastered people skills--or at least a set of people skills that has allowed them to persuade enough people to support them in their career advancement.

Let's pause a moment and consider this.

What would you say are the biggest causes of stress, frustration, and problems in your life? Could it be relationships with people, money, and health (or some combination of these)? As I've learned from my business coach and mentor, Dani Johnson, almost all of our frustrations and anxieties in life stem from one of these three areas. While money and health problems are outside the scope of this book, it's my guess that dealing with people is the single biggest challenge in your life. If so, you're not alone. This is true to some degree in the lives of everyone I know.

Isn't it interesting that, even though these three areas are at the root of almost all of the challenges we face in life, precious little time is spent on developing our skills in any of these area during our formal education years?

How Much Training?

A few years ago, I was caught exceeding the speed limit in the United Kingdom. At the time, if you were caught exceeding the speed limit by less than ten percent, there was an opportunity to avoid having three penalty points added to your driving license if you agreed to attend a half-day speed awareness seminar. That sounded fair, so off I went to attend the seminar.

I must admit that it was actually a very good seminar and I ended up learning quite a lot. But the most interesting part of the seminar was right in the beginning when they asked us to split into groups of fifteen to twenty people and to do an exercise where each group totals up the number of years' worth of driving experience we had in the group.

All the groups responded in turn, and the numbers sounded impressive.

The groups all returned numbers of three hundred years or more worth of driving experience. Then the seminar leader asked us to do a second exercise. This time, we had to total up the number of days' worth of driving instruction we had all received. The point came across clearly. Most groups had as little as thirty days' worth of driving instruction. No wonder there was so much room for improvement in all our respective driving skills.

Why do I tell you this story? Because the same thing happens during my training seminars when I ask participants to total up the number of years' worth of formal education they participated in and then ask them to compare that number to the total time they've invested in learning about people, communication, negotiation, conflict resolution, and persuasion.

By the time you add up the years spent in grade school, high school, college, and on the job, most people will have participated in anywhere form twelve to twenty years in formal education, without having spent a single day learning about people.

No wonder, then, that the negotiation results obtained by business people across the world are so consistently mediocre. What little skill they have revolves around finding manipulative means to get their own way.

A Huge Opportunity For Someone

There is a profound opportunity awaiting negotiators who will equip themselves with the tools to approach their negotiations by design rather than just reacting by default to the negotiation scenarios that play out around them every day.

The complexity that has been added to our world because of globalization and the rapid improvement of communication technologies (our connectedness) means that those who understand and apply the best practices (and indeed the leading practices that support negotiating in a business context) will get an unfair share of the spoils that are coming up for grabs.

This new generation of elite business negotiators will go back to basics and rise up to restore honor and integrity to deal-making, operating by the original intent of the word "negotiate" (to do business), rather than merely to "reach agreement" where there are opposing views. They will be confident leaders of teams, able to coach their colleagues and collaborators in the consistent and ever-present application of negotiation best and leading practices.

Becoming aware that you are constantly negotiating will increase your earnings, enhance your relationships, reduce conflict, and maximize your time. As you learn to communicate accurately and convincingly, you will reduce the time you sacrifice on the altar of miscommunication, which inevitably leads to escalation, delays, frustrations, and frayed tempers.

But why would you take my word for it?

Be Highly Selective Which Model You Follow

I've learned that it's important—no, absolutely critical—that you take great care in the selection of whose advice you decide to follow. After all, you will end up with the same results as those whose advice you choose to follow. This requires you to pursue a holistic approach to finding the right counsel.

For instance, if a person offering your advice on how to grow your business is on their third marriage and forsaken by their children, you can reasonably assume that their advice will include working sixteen hours every day and sacrificing your family.

In the same way, you should be cautious about the counsel you seek to improve your negotiation results. It's all well and good to pursue a highly-tactical approach to negotiations, but be prepared that you may end up sacrificing long-term relationships on the altar of short-term gains.

What Qualifies Me To Teach This?

To help professionals reach an elite level of negotiation capability, I've spent (as of this writing) more than twenty years studying, specializing in, and applying negotiation best and leading practices:

- I completed a two year executive MBA with a major in negotiation skills under the leadership and supervision of Professor Manie Spoelstra.

- I've participated in the forums created for the teaching of negotiation skills by the traditionally-recognized centers of excellence in negotiation—the likes of the Project on Negotiation at Harvard University, Wharton, Oxford, Essec's IRENE (Institute for Research and Education on Negotiation) and others.

- I've read the books written by both pretenders and conquerors.

- I've internalized the biographies and autobiographies of those who have been widely recognized as great negotiators, including Nelson Mandela, Henry Kissinger, and Margaret Thatcher.

- I've also cast the net wider and made an in-depth study of communication skills, psychology and the characteristics that underpin elite-level performance in the domains of business, politics, arts and sports.

Driven by a passion for negotiation as the oil that greases the wheels of commerce, I've dedicated my career to the pursuit of restoring honor and integrity to the art of deal-making in the business world and equipping business people with the practical, proven tools they need to negotiate their way through the complex globalized world that we live in today.

Since 2003, I've trained more than 10,000 business people in 60 countries (typically in small group based seminars of ten to sixteen people per group), and I've negotiated on-camera with more than 3,500 business negotiators, providing them with individual feedback benchmarked against our database of best practices.

I've helped Fortune 500-level executives shape strategic negotiation approaches and craft processes that incorporate best practices to support their teams.

I've coached CEO's, Company Presidents, and Vice Presidents on their personal negotiation approaches.

I've equipped professional buyers with the tools they need to pursue discrete and different approaches to different categories and classes of suppliers as well as set them up to succeed in the critical area of internal company negotiations.

I've empowered sellers with the strategies, tactics, and techniques needed to deal with both the business side for their clients, as well as effectively handle the negotiations with professional procurement departments.

I've worked with (and continue to work with) some of the biggest organizations, companies, and most recognizable brands in the world. Our Advanced Negotiation Academy Seminars and our Masters Negotiation Academy Seminars set the standard in business negotiation.

It was never my intent to build the biggest negotiation skills development organization in the world, only to build the best.

Indulge me for a moment and think about the best hamburger you ever had. Where did you buy it? I would bet you didn't buy it at one of the global burger chains. You probably bought it at a local neighborhood restaurant. You see, even though the large national and global burger chains can serve you an adequate burger because they've standardized and scaled their operations, they are not in the business of building the best hamburgers out there. This has always been our philosophy—to build the very best company in our industry, not necessarily the biggest.

With Great Success, Great Failure

Before you think it has all been effortless and without blemish, I should also point out to you that along the way I've had my misfortunes and misadventures. I've had to deal with failed partnerships, being embezzled and not starting my business life equipped with the right skills to manage relationships and the rapid growth of a dynamic business. I spent so much time focused on satisfying the needs of our clients that I neglected the proper structures that needed to be in place to duplicate myself.

I also spent way too much time learning only about negotiation and neglected to invest in my own continuous personal development in the areas of relationships, finance, parenting, and time management. Making mistakes can be humbling, but it positions you to learn…if you are open to it. I wasn't always so inclined, but the way I think now is to analyze the mistakes I've made with a view to making them "pay forward." I do whatever I can to avoid making the same mistakes again, and I count the cost of those mistakes as "tuition fees" for the education I received from them.

A Modern Dilemma

It's time that we get intentional about the way we negotiate. Why is it that our hyper-connected world has not brought us the improvement in relationships that were promised by the prospect of being connected at all times? Why is it that a handshake is no longer sufficient to close an agreement? Why is there so little trust in the business world?

It seems as if our global connectedness has also brought with it some side effects that are not very desirable. In the arena of big business, it's become acceptable to renege on agreements, to find loopholes to get out of agreements that are no longer desirable and to display adversarial behavior that does not respect the dignity of others.

As I've gone around the world, I've both encountered and heard stories with metronomic regularity about interactions with negotiation counterparts that are, quite frankly, way out of line. Global business relationships and transactions demand a rigorous and robust approach that maintains validity across all geographies and cultures. Working in partnership with institutions like the European Business School in Germany, the University College Cork, and executives in Fortune 500 and FTSE 100 companies, we have developed what we believe to be the world's most robust and effective business negotiation methodology.

Why This Book?

I am writing this book to equip you with the negotiation strategies, tools, tactics, and techniques you will need to succeed in business negotiations without having to sacrifice your relationships, health, or integrity. Much has been written about negotiation from different perspectives, ranging from ivory tower academics to the tactical, "dog-eat-dog" trenches of retail and labor relations. What I've never encountered is a book written from a perspective of moving you from your default negotiation style to an intentional negotiation approach.

I've never encountered a book that human nature tells us what need to know about negotiation. After all, since we all belong to the human race, we can use what we know about human nature to find commonalities to build agreement, rather than taking a view that negotiation is about resolving some kind of conflict between the protagonists.

Three Key Arguments

This book sets out three key arguments.

- Your ability to negotiate effectively in all spheres of your life has a far greater impact on your quality of life than you have probably ever realized.

- It is your preferences (what you like to do) and not your competencies (what you are capable of doing) that will determine the results of your negotiations.

- Consistently applying some simple best practices to your business negotiations can deliver astonishing results.

If any of these points seem new or interesting to you it is probably because, like most people, you tend to think of negotiation as something formal that takes place around a table in a formal setting.

It is true that we live in a world where specialization is highly valued. Your contribution to any business is measured by doing a specific set of tasks consistently at a determined level of competence. The truth is, negotiation is required whenever there is an unmet need in evidence.

The Promise Of This Book

In this book, I will:

- present you with a framework that you can use to bring structure to your negotiation preparations

- equip you with the same strategies, tactics, techniques, and tools we teach to our corporate clients

- provide a simple but effective Negotiation Preparation Checklist which will help you ensure that you consistently apply negotiation best practices to your daily deal making

The 4 Pillars of Negotiation

The book has been broken down into four parts, each centered around one of the four pillars of business negotiation: Vision, Value, Process, and Relationships.

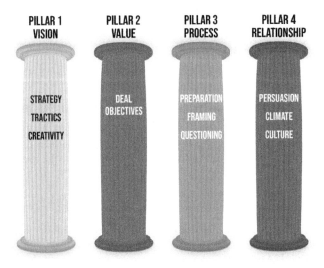

THE FOUR PILLARS OF LEADING PRACTICE BUSINESS NEGOTIATION

PILLAR 1 VISION	PILLAR 2 VALUE	PILLAR 3 PROCESS	PILLAR 4 RELATIONSHIP
STRATEGY	DEAL OBJECTIVES	PREPARATION	PERSUASION
TRACTICS		FRAMING	CLIMATE
CREATIVITY		QUESTIONING	CULTURE

In Part I, we will examine the Vision for deal-making. This includes the importance of understanding who all the stakeholders are, what motivates them, and how to identify if there are any common interests that can be uncovered to not only claim value but create value. We will look at the five fundamental negotiation strategies available to you and your counterparts. Ensuring that you select the most appropriate negotiation strategy will go a long way toward shortening the length of the deal cycle and will send a clear signal of your intent. We will end Part I by examining the thirty most commonly used negotiation tactics. We will set you up with all you need to know to both use and counter ninety-nine percent of the negotiation tactics you are likely to encounter in the global commercial environment. Part I is the "why" behind the deal.

In Part II, we will dive into understanding the Value of the transaction from the perspective of all the stakeholders. We will unpack how to set specific objectives for your negotiations in a way that will significantly increase your likelihood of getting results that meet your expectations, while at the same time satisfying your counterpart's needs. There is some science specific to trading concessions. We will provide insight into setting up deals and proactively managing the satisfaction level of all parties. Part II is the "who" behind the deal.

Part III deals with managing the Process of negotiation and ensuring that you control as much of the deal-making as is possible. Negotiating on behalf of an organization also means that you may find yourself part of a negotiating team—maybe even leading one. This adds significant potential complexity which you need to address in a structured, effective way. Part III analyzes this "how" behind the deal.

Lastly, Part IV will focus on Relationship aspects of negotiation. Here, we will equip you with the insights and skills you need to pro-actively manage the negotiation environment. We will end by setting you up with the keys to persuasively communicate your arguments, even in a cross-cultural setting. This section is the heart of negotiation—the "who."

If you have an open mind for new ideas and seek to move your negotiation results to the next level, this book will offer simple, proven, effective, and high-impact strategies, techniques and tactics to zoom right past your objectives.

Let's get started.

Chapter One: The Slow, Agonized Death of Negotiation

Executive Summary

- The original meaning of the word "negotiation" has been distorted over time, to the detriment of many facets of business.

- Due to the complexities of human interactions, there is no "one-size-fits-all" step-by-step process for engaging in negotiation.

- There are six characteristics that top negotiators exhibit: people skills, teachability, courage, ambition, consistency, and fun.

Negotiation Isn't Really Changing...But It Is

Few activities in business are done as often (or as poorly) as negotiation.

There are negotiations taking place in every workplace around the world every day. Whether you think so or not, I'm one hundred percent sure that you've been party to a considerable number of negotiations throughout your career to date, not least of which is the negotiation that resulted in you earning what you are currently making.

Of all the negotiations that you've observed or participated in, how many would you say were memorable, effective, efficient, and delivered the intended results measured over the long term? I would guess that only a handful of negotiations truly delivered on your expectations over time.

Add to that the increasingly global world we live in today and the growing evidence that big corporations are blazing a trail in being unreliable and untrustworthy in their business dealings at an ever-accelerating rate. Disappointingly, a handshake is no longer good enough to seal a deal.

Unfortunately, the art of honorable deal-making (negotiating) seems to be dying a slow death. As a matter of fact, since the turn of the century, I've observed a sharp increase in the number of large organizations that say their counterparts are no longer respecting their written contracts. Granted, this tendency may be more prevalent in some industries than in others, but I've encountered this issue in just about every industry and in every country where I've consulted or trained.

It seems that in this age of large and powerful organizations, commitment to maintain and adhere to agreements is no longer held up as an admirable and ethical quality. Within the corporate business environment, many seem to view negotiation skills as tools to support the exploitation and manipulation of others; a means to bend suppliers, buyers, and other stakeholders to your will.

Publicly-traded companies almost always focus most of their energy and resources on the growth that can be achieved in the next quarter and the next financial year. While this is important, in the absence of a strong culture of business ethics, it can create an environment where negotiators are incentivized to forsake the long-term strategic perspective (i.e., protecting and cultivating the business relationship and long term profitability) for a short-term game of tactical negotiation plays (i.e., getting the upper hand).

Within professional purchasing departments, success is generally measured by how much money was saved during the current financial year as measured against what was spent during the previous fiscal year, per category. On the sales side, the pressure to meet quarterly revenue and margin targets is unrelenting. Combine these two perspectives, and it is no wonder that both buyers and sellers tend toward tactical and manipulative approaches to serve the achievement of their short-term interests and objectives.

While parties all along the buy/sell spectrum are fond of talking about Total Cost of Ownership (TCO), that is seldom what drives decision making. Both buyers and sellers are typically incentivized to achieve yearly targets rather than targets that match the TCO considerations.

Within this sea of distrust and manipulative negotiation tactics, there are, thankfully, some very prominent islands of honorable negotiation excellence. I've had the pleasure to meet many senior business leaders who have not only expressed their desire to conduct business honorably but have actually backed up their passion with transparent processes and accountability within their departments and organizations. I believe there is a growing number of people and organizations that recognize the value of building business value on the back of old-fashioned deal-making values like trust, integrity, transparency, mutual benefit, and a focus on sustainable long-term relationships.

For far too long, negotiation training and skills development have been presented almost like a 'dark art' or a mystic capability by both academic institutions and traditional negotiation skills training companies alike.

The Hundred-Year Transition

Anthropologists tell us that one of the main distinctions between the society we live in today versus only seventy to a hundred years ago is the fact that we are mostly an urban population now and we have built massive public and private sector organizations that simply didn't exist in previous generations. We have mostly moved on from an agricultural society to a metropolitan society. There are several organizations in the world today that employ more than a million people. The likes of the U.S. Department of Defense, Walmart, The National Health Service (NHS) in the United Kingdom, and The China National Petroleum Corporation all employ well over a million people, to name but a few.

Interestingly, the largest businesses make up only a tiny percentage of the total number of companies registered in the USA. In 2012, according to U.S. Census Bureau data:

- There were 5.73 million employer firms in the U.S.

- Firms with fewer than 500 workers accounted for 99.7 percent of those businesses.

- Businesses with less than 20 workers made up 89.6 percent.

Against this backdrop, roughly 38% of the workforce in the USA work for large corporations. This means that only a tiny percentage of corporations employ a vast portion of the workforce. These relatively few, super-sized organizations are tremendously influential in the ways they shape the world around us. They spend massive sums on influencing their customers, governments, and the environment around them.

The growth of these super-large organizations has had a profound impact on the prevailing view of negotiation. As organizations grow ever-larger, they need more processes and specialization in functional disciplines to remain effective. So, what has happened over the years is that employees have been put in positions where their role has been defined functionally (e.g., Human Resources, Legal, Accounting, Sales, Purchasing, and Logistics). In turn, this has resulted in people no longer understanding that the act of doing business means that you are negotiating. Most modern thinking around sales and purchasing relegates negotiation to being only one step of the purchasing or sales process, rather than a process itself.

In reality, purchasing and sales are subsets of doing business (our definition of negotiation)—not the other way around.

It certainly appears that a linear approach to negotiation seems to have become the favored approach because this chimes with the process-driven, functional discipline focused construction of most large organizations.

This Way Of Thinking Is Hurting Business

As a result of this transition to a myopic, segmented approach to doing business, most business-related negotiations fail to deliver full value to the participants. Because so few organizations recognize that the very act of doing business day-to-day involves negotiation, significant value escapes throughout the deal-making process.

If you have been thinking of negotiation as an event rather than a process, I have great news for you; there is a substantial opportunity for you to dramatically improve the results from your and your organization's deal-making efforts.

I've had the opportunity to work with thousands of business people, and most are reactive in their approach to negotiation—they negotiate by default rather than by design. They think of negotiation primarily as a means of resolving conflict, and "win-win" scenarios, and therefore are not adequately prepared to engage in negotiation in a structured and measurable way. They have not harnessed the power of consistently applying negotiation best practices in support of the functional discipline (purchasing, sales, legal, mergers, and acquisitions, etc.) they represent.

Through consistently applying the approach that I will be laying out in this book, you are going to realize a significant improvement in your and your organizations' negotiation outcomes. It is time to go back to basics and adopt a fundamental approach to negotiation that will help you to profitably and economically navigate the global, cross-cultural environment where we do business today.

It is time to implement a process of negotiating (doing business) that not only focuses on claiming value, but also on creating value.

It is time to recognize the timeless value of relationships and their role as the ultimate enabler of deal-making success.

It is time to recognize and respond intentionally to tactical approaches to negotiation, rather than react to them.

It is time to start negotiating by design rather than by default.

Airplanes, Golf, and Linear Solutions

Picture this scenario: you're leading a team that has been tasked to take apart the world's largest passenger aircraft, the Airbus A380, transport it to a different location and then to reassemble it. Do you think this would be a challenging task? Of course! You will have to keep track of millions of parts and you will have to develop a process for the project that will ensure compliance with rigorous standards.

Even though this would be a mammoth task to accomplish, it is at least theoretically possible, due to the linear relationship between the parts of the airplane. In other words, you should be able (with the help of several professionals) to come up with a linear, sequential process both to deconstruct and reassemble the airplane. We know this is possible because we know that the airplane was built according to a linear and sequential process.

Now, let me present you with a completely different kind of challenge: the challenge of hitting a golf ball.

I grew up in Johannesburg, South Africa, and had the opportunity to play lots of golf, due to the abundance of golf courses and excellent weather conditions. I'm certainly not an accomplished golfer, but I have played enough golf to know that it is a complex game with many variables.

Let's say you were a professional golfer, and I asked you to hit a golf ball down the fairway. You hit a great shot. Then I challenge you to hit another shot, but this time I would like you to duplicate the result of the first shot exactly. In other words, I would like you to hit the ball in such a way as to ensure that it ends up in the exact same spot as your first shot.

What do you think is the likelihood of being able to achieve this outcome? Pretty slim. You see, golf is an excellent example of a complex activity that cannot be duplicated exactly due to its many variables, just as assembling an aircraft is an excellent example of an activity that can be duplicated because it can be reduced to a linear sequence of steps with limited variables.

Think about the variables that will have an impact on where your ball ends up when you hit that second ball. The wind speed and direction, your stance when addressing the ball, your grip on the golf club, the height you hit the ball, whether it lands on a soft or hard patch of ground, and the amount of spin on the ball. The odds that you will be able to get the ball to end up in the same spot as your first shot are infinitesimally small.

Because golf is complex, it is not useful to create an approach to getting around the golf course linearly and sequentially. But for the sake of discussion, what might it look like if you were to apply a linear and sequential approach to golf?

You have fourteen clubs in your bag, including the putter. To hit the ball a long distance, you use one of your "woods" which are the clubs that hit the ball low, enabling it to travel a long distance. At the other end of the scale, you have "short irons," which are used for hitting the ball a shorter distance, at a higher trajectory, with greater accuracy. If you were to follow a linear approach to getting the ball in the hole on a par five, it would look something like this:

- Start by hitting with your driver.
- Hit the next shot with the three wood.
- Hit the next shot with the five wood.
- Hit the next shot with the three iron.
- Choose smaller clubs until you get to the putter at the end.

Anyone who has ever played a round of golf would tell you that this would be a completely ridiculous way to play golf and that you would be out on the golf course for a very long time, trying to get the ball in the hole.

A far more effective way to play is to examine the lie of the ball, identify the target area where you would like the ball to end up, assess the weather and ground conditions, and consider your strengths and weaknesses as a player (you likely get better, more consistent results playing with certain clubs than with others). Based on that information (and your instincts) you would decide which golf club would be best suited to deliver the desired result.

Apply This Principle To Negotiation

Let's bring this back to negotiation.

Negotiation happens between people, and people are complex beings, not linear and sequential beings. It seems very strange to me that anyone would want to approach people—or indeed, the topic of negotiation—linearly and sequentially, but most people do.

While we know that certain things work better with all people (for instance treating your counterparts with dignity, honor, and respect) and that therefore it is a good idea to make these things a part of our standard repertoire, we should not conclude that our standard approaches will work equally well in every instance, across cultures and geographies.

The bottom line is that it would not make sense to come up with a linear, three-step, four-step, five-step (or any number of steps) negotiation program. But this is precisely what almost all leading universities and negotiation skills training providers advocate.

I believe the philosophy behind this approach stems from the process-based thinking that has infiltrated every area of big business. A linear approach could maybe work in a monocultural, one-dimensional, straightforward type of negotiation, but is impractical for extracting the best deal in a complex, multi-cultural business environment. It doesn't make sense that you would break down negotiation into a series of steps, such as:

1. Preparing.

2. The opening statement of positions.

3. Exploring interests.

4. Making concessions (bargaining).

5. Closing.

You may find yourself in a different culture where the parties are unwilling to state positions or begin bargaining until after you've established a trusted relationship. If you were to follow your linear, five- or six-step process to negotiation in that scenario, you might well find yourself out on the sidewalk very early on in the deal.

It is far more useful to follow a due-diligence-based approach to negotiation (like golf), where you assess the demands of each situation and then decide on the best path to pursue, based on a thorough checklist of best and leading practices.

How It Benefits You

If you understand that there is no one correct way to approach all negotiations—just as there is no one standard way to hit every golf ball on every course—but that to be a successful negotiator demands the implementation and use of different strategies and supporting tactics, then you will produce a significantly higher level of results from your negotiations.

If you understand that your default preferences, competencies, and behaviors will be appropriate in many deal-making environments, but not in all deal-making environments, then you set yourself up to negotiate by design instead of by default. Negotiating by design is what separates those who are good from those who are great.

You have to move away from negotiating in reaction to your counterpart as a result of the universal principle of reciprocity that underpins human nature. The principle of reciprocity simply states that we return to others the form of behavior that they demonstrate towards us (more about this later). You see, if you let your approach to any negotiation be determined by the approach that your counterpart is pursuing, rather than be determined by the correct approach based on the demands of the particular type of negotiation that you're involved in, then you will never truly be able to reach an elite level of negotiation competence.

Characteristics of Successful Negotiators

What is required to be an exceptional business negotiator? What are the trademarks of those that are unusually successful at deal making?

Over the past twenty years, I've studied, researched, and interviewed some of the leading negotiators in the world—some of them icons in their field. I've studied successful business leaders, athletes, and artists, and I've come up with a list of six characteristics that are shared by all who have achieved extraordinary results in their field. These characteristics are indicative of success in the business negotiation world as well.

Characteristic #1: Unusual People Skills

Success in business requires you to be skilled in dealing with people. Of the six characteristics that I will list here, this is the only one that is specific to negotiation and doing business. The other five characteristics you can apply to anything, from weightlifting to losing weight. But to get to the top in business, you will need the support of others.

Opportunity comes from people, money comes from people, problems come from people, and help comes from people. Without the cooperation and support of others, it simply will not be possible for you to reach the top of the ladder. Without the people skills necessary to win others over to support you in the achievement of your vision and goals it will be a very long, hard slog to the top—if it is even possible at all.

There are plenty of examples of people who are brilliant but simply did not have the people skills necessary to get others to support their ideas. It is certainly possible to have a successful career without excellent people skills in some technical environments, but it will be almost impossible to have successful, lasting, and mutually fulfilling relationships with your family, colleagues, and other stakeholders if you are not skilled at dealing with people. You may be able to achieve results in one dimension without excellent people skills, but it will be impossible for you to lead a holistically successful life.

Having great people skills requires you to have an in-depth understanding of a few critical things about people, starting with yourself:

- You must recognize the strengths and weaknesses of your character and personality.

- You must embrace the fact that not all people are motivated by the same interests.

- You must learn about and accept human nature and use this information to motivate people by communicating persuasively.

While different interests motivate people, we are all joined together by similar desires (irrespective of gender, culture, or religion). Awareness of that truth is the fuel that propelled the all-time greats like Abraham Lincoln, Nelson Mandela, Mahatma Gandhi, and Martin Luther King. These world-changers realized the power in harnessing one of the essential principles in the context of deal making—the universal Rule of Reciprocity that underpins human nature and all behavior.

A Key To Good People Skills: Understanding Reciprocity

The principle of reciprocity states that we return to others the form of behavior they exhibit toward us. If I greet you respectfully and politely, the likelihood of you responding the same way is pretty good. Similarly, if I welcome you in a manner that is rude and curt, then I can also reasonably expect the same behavior in return. If you discriminate against me and hate me because of my racial background, then you can reasonably expect that I would treat you in the same way.

It is wholly expected behavior to respond to others in the same way that they treated you. It is also the hallmark of personal mediocrity.

One of the critical attributes these great world-changers had in common was the ability—and the will—to treat others as they decided to treat them, based on their own convictions, rather than mirroring how they were being treated. Put another way; they consciously violated the principle of reciprocity by not responding in kind to how their adversaries were treating them.

If you always reciprocate what others do to you, you will always have the little you have. But if you can give people what they want, regardless of how they treat you, then they will do whatever they can to help you get what you want.

Characteristic #2: Teachability

Top performers are teachable.

When you look at top performers in almost any discipline (e.g., sports, arts, politics, business, etc.), you will notice that advisors, coaches, and consultants almost always surround them. They recognize the power of submitting themselves to instruction and correction; they have concluded that it is a necessary condition for sustained success to rely on the counsel of others. What I've noticed is that the lower down you go in an organization, the more resistant people tend to be to correction and feedback.

The fact that you are reading this book is an indication that you are teachable and looking for counsel on improving your results.

It has been said that repetition is the mother of skill. Unfortunately, in the western world, we've developed a view that, once we've completed our formal schooling and education, we are done with learning, released to focus on deploying our skills. In practical terms, this means that when most people have attended a seminar on presentation skills, sales skills, or improving their negotiation skills, they assume that they've now mastered the content and its application and they become closed to further developing their skill sets in these topic areas.

You would never see someone who wishes to be a concert pianist quit taking piano lessons after a couple of months, assuming that they have developed a world class level of skill. No, they will combine ongoing lessons, coaching, and practice to develop and hone their skills continuously. Top-level performers know that it is not intensity, but consistency that delivers winning results. You can't attend a two-day leadership seminar and then expect to be a great leader. You have to apply the habits of great leadership daily to be a great leader.

This is the difference between professionals at the top of their game and pretenders.

I have a confession to make in this area. For many years, I invested heavily in learning everything I could about negotiation skills. I read just about every book I could find on the topic, completed a two-year course of study under Professor Manie Spoelstra, and attended training seminars offered by the world's leading academic institutions in both the USA and Europe. But my motivation was to find the evidence to validate what I believed would be the critical elements to negotiation success, rather than have an open mind to learn about negotiation from those who had a record of success in this area.

While I saw negotiation skills as a strategic—albeit highly-specialized—skill, I didn't recognize that the very academic institutions that promoted their research on negotiation often didn't understand that negotiation was simply "doing business." Because I was only focused on learning from traditional institutions that were part of the "negotiation establishment," my thinking was clouded by the assumption that negotiation was really only a means to find the middle ground between conflicting positions.

It turns out that, until about seven years ago (from the date of writing), I wasn't motivated to be teachable outside my areas of preference. I wasn't willing to put myself into a position of discomfort (a necessary condition for learning).

Then I met my coach and mentor, Dani Johnson, and I chose to become teachable. My whole life has been transformed significantly for the better since I made that decision. While the subject of this book does not necessarily warrant a discussion of my personal background, it is worth noting that since I decided to start learning from the best I've managed to transform my failing marriage into a thriving partnership, my poor parenting into fulfilling relationships with my children, my faltering health to vibrant vitality, and my debt-ridden financial affairs into a debt free, financially independent environment. Take advice from results.

Characteristic #3: Courage

Can you think of one person in all of history who has achieved superlative or laudable results from doing average things? It's simply not possible. If you only do what everyone else does, you're only going to get the same results everybody else gets.

But what happens to you when you swim upstream? What happens to you when you go against conventional wisdom? You get resistance. It may be subtle, or it may be confrontational. You may provoke the ire of people you respect. You may face public rejection. You may find yourself abandoned or admonished by good friends. These are the times when you must have courage.

On the face of it, this idea may seem counterintuitive. It might appear to be in your best interest to continue doing things the way everyone else does rather than set yourself up for opposition. But that's not how anyone achieves greatness in anything.

If you've spent any time with me, you'll know that I refer to Nelson Mandela frequently. In my opinion, he is the most accomplished negotiator in modern history.

A little known fact is that South Africa's white apartheid government was the only government ever in recorded history that negotiated themselves out of power. Nelson Mandela was, without a shadow of a doubt, the central and principal architect of the negotiation process that made this miracle happen. This is one of the reasons why Nelson Mandela is revered around the world.

Do you know what his biggest problem was? Convincing his own stakeholders that his approach to the negotiations for a new, democratic South Africa was worth supporting. They thought he'd gone crazy. They challenged him: how can you be conciliatory toward these people who kept you in jail twenty-seven years? What he did was completely counterintuitive, and that was his advantage, but more about that later.

He received the admiration of the world because he was willing to reject conventional wisdom, and he violated the principle of reciprocity. At the same time, he also knew how to invoke and harness the principle of reciprocity. More on that later, too.

Whether you intend to be a world-class negotiator or the best mom you know how to be, to be successful, you must be willing to not do what everyone else is doing, and that requires courage.

Characteristic #4: Ambition

Another characteristic of the most successful negotiators is heightened ambition. It's not possible for you to achieve elite level results if you don't demand great results of yourself. You don't win an Olympic medal by sleeping late, overeating, and partying. Ambition and discipline must go hand-in-hand, or you will spend your life frustrated. Ambitious people are prepared to pay the price that other people are not willing to pay. That's how you get better results.

Too often, our culture associates ambition with greed or ruthlessness. In the movies, ambitious people are often shown without a moral/ethical compass that would prevent them from harming others on their way to the top. While ambition drives people to do whatever it takes to achieve their goals, character (hopefully) prevents them from doing malevolent or unethical things in that pursuit.

Top achievers always reach for more—no matter how high they go in their pursuits. It's the same in negotiation: if you want a better deal, you need to be willing to ask for a better deal. You have to do the bargaining. It won't happen any other way. It is not going to get handed to you.

Characteristic #5: Consistency

Success is never sudden; it's always built little by little. Have you heard the expression, "practice makes perfect?" The wisdom behind that proverb is that the consistent, disciplined repetition of a skill creates grooves in the brain, or what athletic trainers call "muscle memory." NBA legends like Larry Bird and Stephan Curry became the best at their game through their relentless, unwavering discipline to consistently practice the fundamentals.

You become a great negotiator through the consistent application of the fundamentals. Now, don't read that to mean that negotiation is a linear and sequential process that can be thoughtlessly repeated in any situation, far from it. However, the skills of negotiation planning, strategy, and tactics can and must be applied with consistency to achieve mastery.

How will you recognize mastery? Basic management theory teaches us that it is not possible to improve something unless you measure it. Think about the great Jamaican Olympic runner Usain Bolt. When training, he wouldn't ever say, "Coach, I felt fast today. I'm sure I was faster than yesterday." No, they objectively compare his results against his previous performance in hard numbers and let the numbers tell them whether or not he is improving.

Whenever I work with companies—anywhere in the world—one of my favorite questions to ask is, "Do you think that you are good negotiators?" Regardless of whether they answer "yes" or "no," nine times out of ten, they can't validate their response because they have no systems in place to track and measure their performance.

Now, I might get a rebuttal like this from a buyer: "We can measure our results: our expense numbers show that we have spent less than last year." But does that number take into account the complexities of the market?

Measuring negotiation results is more complicated than merely comparing this year's numbers to last year's numbers.

What does this mean in the context of negotiation? It means structure. You can't force structure into the negotiation itself, but you can apply a system to your preparations. Systems make your preparation process repeatable. That allows you to track inconsistencies in your preparation and positively iterate your approach little by little.

Characteristic #6: Fun

The final characteristic of successful negotiators—and this is the litmus test in many ways—is that you can have fun while you are negotiating.

How much fun you are having will tell you immediately where you sit on the spectrum of skill mastery. Mastery is reflected through fun. Referring again to Olympian Usain Bolt, you don't see him dragging himself out of bed, murmuring, "Got to run that bloody hundred meter final today," or "Goodness, it's the Olympic Games again," or "Ugh…drudgery and death." No, when he gets the opportunity to participate in the Olympic Games, it is the moment that he's been living for.

The same can be said of performers like U2 or the Rolling Stones. When they play their set before a stadium of screaming fans, they aren't struggling to remember their chords. It is obvious they are having fun because they have mastered the fundamentals of their art.

If you look at negotiation as a chore, you probably haven't mastered it yet. If you get excited at an opportunity to negotiate, it's a good indicator that this is a skill that you've successfully developed. Your consistency to practice the skills of negotiation has brought you to a place of confidence, and confidence makes the process fun.

Are They All Evident In Your Work?

You likely have evidence of all six characteristics working in your negotiations, so to show what it looks like when they aren't working, I'll use myself as an example.

Basically, up until seven years ago (at the time of writing), I was not as teachable as I should have been. That was something that had to change in me significantly. Sure, I had achieved considerable knowledge in the context of corporate negotiations, but there were many other areas of my life where I was simply unteachable. My life has transformed since I changed that.

To put it bluntly, being unteachable is a character flaw. Heightened ambition has never been an issue for me. Courage comes easily. I always have fun doing this. But if I'm frank with myself, where I still catch myself coming up short is in the area of consistency.

Success comes through consistency: practicing the fundamentals (doing the right things), little by little, every day. That's what gets you ahead. It's not that big flash-in-the-pan thing. It's as true in the world of negotiation as any other skill. If you don't do something regularly to improve your ability, it's not going to improve. The problem is, as studies have shown, that only ten percent of people that interact with new knowledge will employ it. Will you be one that applies what you learn in this book or one who peruses it and immediately forgets it?

The choice is yours.

Key Takeaways from Chapter One

- Negotiation happens every day in your workplace, whether you recognize it or not.

- A gradual transition in the common understanding of the word "negotiation" has relegated it to a specific step of a sales or purchasing process.

- Sales and purchasing are subsets of the process of negotiation.

- Negotiation is a complex process, similar to golf, and trying to shoehorn it into a step-by-step process is counterproductive to success.

- There is no one "right way" to engage in negotiation.

- There are six characteristics common among top negotiators (five are common among top performers in any discipline):

  o People Skills: top performers can respectfully interact with people who have different priorities, values, and strengths from themselves.

  o Teachability: top performers are always open to learning from others, and submit themselves to the guidance of experts.

  o Courage: to be successful, you must be willing to do things differently from what others do, even in the face of resistance.

  o Ambition: ambitious people do whatever is necessary to achieve their goals.

  o Consistency: disciplined repetition of fundamental skills produces excellent performance.

  o Fun: if you're not having fun, it is evidence that you haven't mastered the fundamentals of your game.

"There is no passion to be found playing small—in settling for a life that is less than the one you are capable of living."

—Nelson Mandela

Apply It To Your Situation

1. Identify three things you learned from this chapter that you want to begin implementing in your negotiations. Highlight the one you want to do first.

    _____

    _____

    _____

    _____

2. Describe how you see the Six Characteristics of Negotiation Success operating in your life.

    _____

    _____

    _____

    _____

3. Describe an area of your life where you would like to see more of one of the Six Characteristics in operation.

    _____

    _____

    _____

    _____

4. What did you learn about negotiation in this chapter that surprised or enlightened you?

    _____

    _____

    _____

    _____

Chapter Two: Preferences

Executive Summary

- You have a natural negotiation capability, which is a composite of your behaviors, competencies, and preferences.

- Your preferences drive your behavior, not your competencies.

- Preferences fall into four categories that align with the four quadrants of the brain, and their relative strengths and weaknesses.

- Your success as a negotiator is tied directly to your ability to recognize your preferences and honor the preferences of others.

- "Confirmation Bias" is the tendency to limit your acceptance of information to those ideas that align with what you already believe.

Pillar 1: Vision

The first of the four pillars of negotiation is called Vision, and it is primarily concerned with understanding who the stakeholders are, what they value, and what points of agreement you can leverage to create value. We are going to look at some of the psychological underpinnings of everyone at the table, so we can choose strategies, tactics, and techniques to address them accurately later in the book.

But before we can understand our counterparts, we must understand ourselves.

First, Know Thyself

Do you approach all your negotiation opportunities in a standard or similar way? Are you so comfortable with your negotiation approach that you seldom try a new or different approach?

Are your opinions and values sacred and non-negotiable to you, or are you open to new ideas and perspectives when they present themselves?

From our study of negotiation best practices, we have learned that your negotiation capability is a function of three elements:

1. Your behavior.

2. Your competencies or skills.

3. Your preferences.

Among these elements, the most important for us to consider is your preferences.

Preferences Drive Behavior, Not Competencies

Your competency—or ability to do something—is not a very good predictor of your behavior. Think about it: the mere fact that you are capable of doing something does not necessarily mean that you will do it. If we always did what we know to do, we would obey all speed limits, quit smoking, eat five fruits and vegetables every day, and work out for at least thirty minutes, at least three times a week (this is what the experts tell us to do). Instead, our behavior is governed by our preferences.

If you want to predict someone's behavior and adjust your approach to them accordingly, the easiest way is to identify their preferences. What they like to do is a stronger predictor of their behavior than what they know they should do.

In corporate recruitment, potential employees are often subjected to competency-based assessments to determine whether they can do the job they are applying for. This is not a bad idea, but if a preference-based assessment does not augment it, you will have no assurance whatsoever that the job will get done. The fact that you are physically capable of running a marathon does not imply that you will run a marathon. If you do not have a corresponding preference for running a marathon, it is doubtful that you will participate in one.

Over the years, I've encountered many participants in my workshops who tell me that they recognize some of the tools, techniques, and tactics they see demonstrated in the workshop materials. It is, then, fascinating for me to observe them in the negotiation simulations that we use, to see whether they deploy those skills. There is often an "aha" moment when they realize that the fact that they are capable of doing something will not necessarily ensure that they do it.

It is essential for us to identify the preferences we harbor in our approach to negotiation and communication so that we can ensure an holistic engagement rather than remain stuck in our default pathway.

Your preferences will be a combination of "nature" and "nurture." This means that your preferences have been shaped both by your innate qualities and your experiences.

Maybe you were raised by parents who emphasized the value of financial prudence. Or perhaps their focus was on the quality of relationships between family members and friends. Some families value hard work. It could even be that all these things were considered significant.

In addition to this, you may have a natural ability in languages or mathematics that would influence what activities you like to participate in and how you like to spend your free time. These things will also have an impact on your preferences.

Two Sides To Every Brain

In the 1960s, American surgeon, Dr Phillip Vogel performed a series of operations on a group of patients who suffered from severe epileptic seizures. Their condition was so critical that it significantly compromised their lifestyles: they couldn't lead healthy lives.

As a last resort, they experimented with physically separating the left side of these patients' brains from the right side. The theory behind it was that their epilepsy was caused by a storm of brain synapses that started in one half of the brain and spread to the other, sending confusing signals and creating a seizure. To do this, they had to cut through a section of the brain called the corpus callosum—millions of connecting strands between the two halves of the brain. Naturally, they expected there would be side effects, but they were quite surprised by the side effects that manifested.

Dr Roger Sperry conducted a research study on these patients (you can see videos of the experiments on YouTube). Dr Sperry won the 1981 Nobel Prize in Physiology and Medicine for his work with split-brain research.

Dr Sperry discovered that if you physically separate the hemispheres of the brain, you also separate components of the mind. It is akin to saying that if you split the "hardware," you also end up splitting the "software." What it helped him to understand was that different regions of the brain perform different functions, and ultimately, led to the notion of left-brain/right-brain preference.

Preferences and Interests

You've probably heard that it is vital to explore your counterpart's interests when you negotiate. Understanding how interests work is critical to your success in negotiation on any level, and in Chapter 3, we will discuss this in greater detail. For our purposes here, let us establish that interests are the factors that motivate your actions, the stuff behind the positions you take, and the reasons why you do things. You can have an interest in keeping your costs low or for getting preferential treatment in a contract.

There are many different models for considering interests. You may have completed "interest-based" profiles in the past, such as the Myers-Briggs Type Indicator®, the

DISC Assessment®, Insights, Social Styles, and any number of others. All of these models are valid and very useful, but I prefer using a model called the NBI™ (Neethling Brain Instrument) in my workshops because it is simple both to understand and explain in a short time period. The NBI™ is one of several instruments that have been designed based on the research that was pioneered by Dr Roger Sperry.

Most of the other models mentioned before are based on the work done by Carl Jung, the famous Swiss psychologist, and are designed to speak to your personality, which can be time consuming and tricky to work with in cross-cultural contexts, rather than just your preferences, which are more universal. The NBI™ model is culturally-neutral because it's based on the physiological composition of the brain and therefore lends itself to the global audience that we serve. It's simple and appropriate whether you're from Chicago, China, or Chile. There are millions of profiles in the database, so from a statistical validity perspective, it's a pretty robust tool. The important thing is that we have a reference framework that is easy to use and pretty accurate in terms of helping us to understand what motivates people and guides their decision making.

This brings out three key points:

- People may make different decisions based on the same information.

- People may make the same decision for different reasons.

- You will have some preferences and habits that cause you to exercise choices that might be different from the way other people would exercise choices.

It is not useful to think of people as being "right" or "wrong," which is a typical default mindset for most people and limiting to the success of any negotiator.

A New View of Right And Wrong

When I first started traveling outside of my own country and culture, I had what you might call an "awakening." Not in a spiritual sense, but culturally. The first time I went to China and India, I experienced two significant "culture shocks." It would be easy to compare what you see there to what you're accustomed to, and conclude that they're wrong or that our ways are better. You would then be falling back on your comfort with what is familiar over what is unfamiliar.

The more I've traveled, the more I've realized that it is not useful to think of some of the more extreme social differences and customs you experience as wrong or bad; but rather that it is just different.

The same thinking applies to preferences. We often think that people who are different from us are wrong and we are right, but that's a very low level of personal development that will hamper your success in working with people.

More on that as we move through later chapters.

NBI™ and You

The NBI™ model is a metaphorical picture of the brain, and the story behind its development is helpful for context. It is a revolutionary battery of instruments, developed by scientist Kobus Neethling and Professor Paul Torrance at the University of Georgia, that strives to develop whole brain thinking in individuals by isolating the functions of the left and right sides of the brain.

The human brain is made up of two halves (hemispheres) that each control the movement and vision on the opposite side of the body. Previous research had found that the brain consists of millions of small cells called neurons, each with its own central nucleus and branches in all directions. Professor Pyotr Anokhin (a student of Pavlov) found that it is not the number of cells that determines intelligence and creativity, but the ability of the neurons to connect to each other, creating new systems and patterns.

The corpus callosum is the bridge between the hemispheres of the brain. It consists of more than two hundred million nerve fibers. Absent this connection, the hemispheres function largely independently of each other. Dr Sperry's research was the first to make it possible to study the unique functions of the two hemispheres.

According to Wikipedia, "Sperry discovered that each hemisphere had its own specialist functions, confirming a hypothesis that had existed for several years." Sperry himself declared, 'Each disconnected hemisphere appears to have a mind of its own.' A very practical example of this came when one of Sperry's patients got involved in an argument with his wife. The patient reached out to grab her with his one hand, but to everyone's surprise, the other hand immediately grabbed the aggressive hand back!

Although the average person is not confronted with this extreme kind of behavior (mainly because our corpus callosum is still in place), it has become clear that most of us prefer the functions and processes of one of the two hemispheres to the other.

Ned Herrmann developed the first four-quadrant instrument in 1981. Herrmann's studies of Sperry's split-brain studies and Paul McLean's Triune Brain Model lead to a combination theory, based on a metaphorical model of four quadrants.

Building on the work of Herrmann and Paul Torrance, Kobus Neethling determined that both the left and right brain processes (as initially categorized by Sperry) could be divided into two definitive categories, effectively dividing the brain into four quadrants.

Between 1988 and 1991, 2,000 adults and 1,500 pupils (with an equal distribution between 10 and 19 years of age) were included in research groups to test Neethling's model. A question with four possible responses was posed to each of the subjects, who then had to arrange their personal thinking preferences from the strongest to the lowest. The choices for each question were based on the thinking processes belonging to the four different quadrants. Neethling found that thinking preferences fell equally into four preference-clusters, corresponding to the four quadrants. Both the validity and reliability levels of each of the quadrants were found to be consistently high.

The Whole Brain Model identifies four quadrants of thinking styles directly related to the specialized thinking structures of the brain and separates our thinking or brain preferences into those four quadrants"

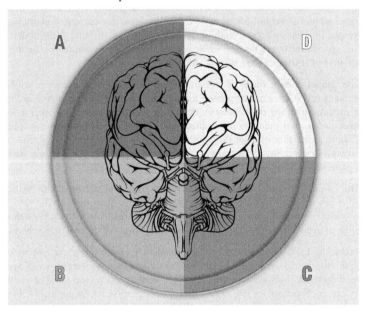

The blue and yellow quadrants represent the top half of the brain (the cortical dimension), while the green and red quadrants represent the bottom half of the brain (the limbic dimension).

The blue and green quadrants represent the left side of the brain. Left-dominant people tend to feel more at ease in technical jobs that require organization, logical reasoning, and a detailed approach. Meanwhile, the yellow and red quadrants represent the right side of the brain. Right-brainers enjoy new ideas and interpersonal involvement.

The NBI™ model categorizes our mental preferences into the following four quadrants:

1. L1, the blue (top-left) quadrant represents the left cortical dimension of the brain, which indicates a preference for rational thinking based on facts. This is the VALUE quadrant.

2. L2, the green (bottom-left) quadrant, represents the left limbic dimension of the brain, which indicates a preference for more in-depth thinking focused on creating and maintaining structure and form. This is the PROCESS quadrant.

3. R2, the red (bottom-right) quadrant, represents the right limbic dimension of the brain, which indicates a preference for more focus on people and feelings. This is the RELATIONSHIP quadrant.

4. R1, the yellow (top-right) quadrant represents the right cortical dimension of the brain, which indicates a preference for innovation, change, and the future. This is the VISION quadrant.

Let's consider each of the quadrants in a little more detail.

To date, millions of people worldwide have completed the NBI™ profile. When we examine the database, it is interesting to note that less than three percent of all those who participated express an equal preference for all four quadrants. Similarly, only three percent of people have a preference for only one of the quadrants.

That leaves us with an overwhelming majority of people who have a preference for either two or three quadrants. That group is split more or less evenly.

This suggests two important considerations that will influence our understanding of the rest of this chapter:

- Humans are complex, multi-faceted beings, each with a unique balance of the four quadrants.

- Viewing people exclusively through the filter of quadrant-based stereotypes is short-sighted and counterproductive for negotiation.

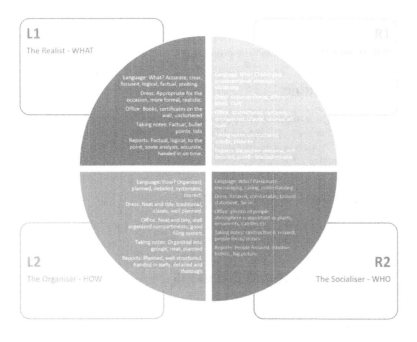

The "Rational One" (A Value Preference)

The L1 (blue) quadrant can be said to represent our "rational self." People with a strong preference in this quadrant tend to lead with facts and figures.

Common Traits

People in the blue quadrant tend to be factual, analytical, accurate, coherent, mathematic, technical, problem-solvers, quantitative, realistic, logical, critical, rational, and sensible. They prefer clarity, focus, concrete values, and well-defined goals.

Management Style

They are typically authoritative, directive, and focused on the task at hand. Often, he or she will gravitate toward the information side of the job (e.g., functions that produce, create, or analyze) as opposed to the management of people. Managers of this type are often content working on problems where they can focus their energy on thinking, processing, and analyzing independently, as opposed to talking through solutions to problems. They live in a rational, technical world where most things can be explained in logical, analytical terms. Opinions, unless backed up with factual evidence, are not important to these people.

Decision Making

People in the blue quadrant make decisions based on facts, analytics, and financial implications. They dig past emotions, opinions, and complexities to the essence of the problem. Their choices are research-based, critical, and technical. They deal with facts in a logical, rational manner, and may force decisions.

Pros and Cons of This Quadrant

The rational thinker has strong analytical, logical skills but can be perceived as aloof, dismissive, and lacking a connection with people.

Typical Blue Quadrant Questions

- Are the facts clear, accurate, and understood?
- Have all the technical specifications been taken into account?
- Is the proposed solution rational?
- Does the research support the decision or way forward?

The "Organized" One (A Process Preference)

The L2 (green) quadrant can be said to represent our "safekeeping self."

Common Traits

People in the green quadrant tend to be controlled, organized, systematic, detailed, punctual, neat, conventional, and traditional. They are often described as practical, reliable, loyal, disciplined, and careful. You will often find them arranging schedules, planning events, organizing materials, or establishing systems. They both implement and follow the rules, regulations, policies, and procedures. They gravitate toward well-proven methods and experience. They prefer to take an orderly, hands-on approach. Whether they are reorganizing their team or their closet, it is purposeful, and the end goal is increased effectiveness and efficiency.

Management Style

Green quadrant types avoid risk as they strive for safety and stability, and tend to resist change. They excel at structure, following procedures, and taking into account all the details necessary to meet deadlines. They like order and work best in an organization where the lines of authority are clear. They are quick to point out faults and administer discipline. They don't like to experiment.

Decision Making

People in the green quadrant make decisions based on precedent, procedures, and rules. They are practical and implement action after extensive planning, testing, and validation. They focus primarily on short-term results because they are usually less risky.

Pros and Cons of This Quadrant

The natural organizer is highly dependable and an excellent project manager, but can be perceived as rigid, inflexible, and controlling.

Typical Green Quadrant Questions

- What is the protocol governing this environment?
- How will we implement and roll out this plan?
- Are all the checks and balances in place?
- Where is the agenda?

The "People" One (A Relationship Preference)

The R2 (red) quadrant can be said to represent our "feeling self."

Common Traits

People in the red quadrant tend to be people-oriented, interpersonal, emotional, spiritual, and supportive. They are often described as sensitive to others, expressive, sociable, and caring. They are collaborators, making sure everyone in the group gets heard. They enjoy team-based environments and projects. Extroverted "reds" tend to be outgoing, expressive, and highly sociable. Introverted "reds" are less expressive, yet equally emotional. They are also highly-intuitive problem-solvers.

Management Style

The red quadrant style of management is highly participative and focused on teams and communities. Managers in this group consider the human resource as the primary asset of the business and are concerned with the organizational climate, policies, and programs that affect employee relationships.

Decision Making

People in the red quadrant make decisions based on emotions and an emphasis on team cooperation. They ask for input, encourage others to share ideas, demand fairness, and consult people close to them before stepping out into a decision. They like to ensure that all stakeholders have been heard.

Pros and Cons of This Quadrant

The people person has excellent networking, people, and relationship skills, but can allow emotions to hinder their view of people and projects.

Typical Red Quadrant Questions

- Have we received input from everyone affected?
- Is the climate (nonverbal) warm and supportive?
- Have all the relationship issues/goals been taken into account?
- Are the relationship and strategic goals balanced?

The "Big Picture" One (A Visionary Preference)

The R1 (yellow) quadrant can be said to represent our "experimental self." People with a strong preference in this quadrant are typically curious, imaginative, entrepreneurial, and future-focused.

Common Traits

People in the yellow quadrant tend to be creative, holistic, and conceptual. They are often described as intuitive, innovative, visionary, big-picture thinkers. They think in pictures, and often have several movies playing in their heads simultaneously. They thrive in unstructured environments with lots of variety and potential risk. They are flexible and adaptable, and they are best leveraged when they can be imaginative and challenge the status quo. These are your strategic vision casters. They tend to be unconventional, spontaneous, and innovative.

Management

The yellow quadrant style of management is holistic, risk-oriented, and adventurous. This is the style of entrepreneurs and leaders who think far into the future. They could be new product developers, super sales people, strategic thinkers, and brainstormers.

Decision Making

People in the yellow quadrant make decisions based on their intuition of the big picture. They speculate, take risks, and try new alternatives. They are exploratory and unconventional. Their process is typically informal ("shoot from the hip") and future-focused. They are risk-takers and explorers.

Pros and Cons of This Quadrant

This visionary is an excellent creative problem-solver, idea-creator, and opportunity-seeker, but often lacks follow-through or great ideas due to a non-preference of detail and execution.

Typical Yellow Quadrant Questions

- What needs to be changed and challenged?
- What is the bigger picture?
- How does this risk bring value?
- What are the creative opportunities?

Negotiating With 'The Whole Brain'

Going back to our circle cut into four quadrants, I would like you to give yourself a score in each quadrant. Imagine that the center of the circle represents zero and the edge of the circle represents ten. In each quadrant, draw a dot that represents how you feel you score. If you feel you are strong the blue quadrant, draw a dot closer to the outer edge; if you feel you are weak in that area, draw a dot nearer to the center of the circle. This same exercise could be done by drawing a circle with vertical and horizontal axes on a sheet of paper.

Now, draw lines to connect the dots so that you create a four-sided shape. It might be a square, but more likely it will be a diamond or trapezoid shape that is long on two sides and short on the others. It should look like something like one of the diagrams below:

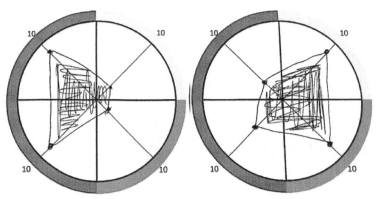

As a fun exercise, have your partner or a friend plot what they think your strong and weak areas are and see if they arrive at the same shape you did.

Different Shapes

The people across the proverbial table from you are individuals, and each one has a unique combination of aspects from each of the four quadrants as individual as their fingerprint. With that in mind, the notion of one-size-fits-all negotiation goes right out the window. Every strategy, tactic, and technique must be agile enough to facilitate a connection with your counterpart that leads to a mutually satisfactory outcome. The most reliable way to ensure the best possible results from your negotiations is to ensure you prepare to offer up something that covers the preferences of all four quadrants. This is where the NBI™ profile presents the perfect negotiation preparation aide.

Let's look at the practical implications for a moment.

Picture someone with whom you have found it very difficult to negotiate. Now, consider the similarities and differences between you and that person, not just in terms of gender and physical appearance, but of temperament, sense of humor, and other preferences as outlined in the NBI™ profile quadrants. What do you recognize about yourself and your thinking and communication preferences when it comes to painful exchanges with your counterpart(s)? If you think back to other challenging relationships that you've had in the past, are you able to identify any trends? Do their preferences fall in the quadrant opposite your strongest quadrant or are they in the same quadrant as yours?

Now picture someone with whom you have found it easy to negotiate. Again, think about the similarities and differences between you and your counterpart. What do you recognize about yourself and your thinking and communication preferences when it comes to enjoyable exchanges with your counterpart(s)? If you think back to other highly productive and agreeable relationships that you've had in the past, are you able to identify any trends?

It has been my experience that most people in a sales role will tend to have stronger preferences for the red and yellow quadrants and those in the position of professional or technical buyers will tend to have stronger preferences in the green and blue quadrants. As you can see, this can easily lead to misunderstandings and challenging negotiations only as a result of the counterparts being motivated by different interests. For you to move to the next level of negotiation competence, you will need to get comfortable with the fact that it is best to serve your counterparts' preferences and needs instead of trying to convince them of the validity and strength of your preferences and supporting arguments. It is the basic law of sowing and reaping.

4 Pillars of Negotiation Best Practice

At this point, I want to introduce one of the foundational concepts in this book. In our research into negotiation best practices, we identified four critical areas of focus that should be addressed in every business negotiation:

1. **Vision:** This is the "WHY" behind the negotiation, a future focus.

2. **Value:** This is the "WHAT" within the negotiation, the deal objective.

3. **Relationships:** This is the "WHO" of the deal, the people factor—both directly and indirectly involved.

4. **Process:** This is the "HOW" factor, the process governing and supporting the negotiation.

These four pillars correspond to the four quadrants of the brain identified by Dr Roger Sperry and built out by Ned Herrmann and Professor Neethling to create a whole-brain framework for planning and conducting negotiations. We will refer to them frequently in the balance of this book.

THE FOUR PILLARS OF LEADING PRACTICE BUSINESS NEGOTIATION

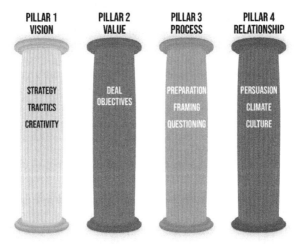

PILLAR 1 VISION	PILLAR 2 VALUE	PILLAR 3 PROCESS	PILLAR 4 RELATIONSHIP
STRATEGY	DEAL OBJECTIVES	PREPARATION	PERSUASION
TRACTICS		FRAMING	CLIMATE
CREATIVITY		QUESTIONING	CULTURE

As you are now aware, each of us will have different preferences with regard to these four key areas, for instance:

- You may prefer to focus on the price and other value elements of negotiations

- You may think that it is more important to focus on innovation and create new options for the future

- You may think that it is all about the people and achieving a harmonious result

- You may feel that due process and attention to detail is the key to negotiation success

Unlikely as it may seem, it is even possible that you could have a preference for all four of the areas mentioned above.

Understand Your Own Preferences

To prepare for the next level of negotiation success, it is imperative that you gain an in-depth understanding of your own thinking and communication preferences. Equally important is to remember that the other people at the table will not necessarily share your preferences, although some will. This does not make them wrong and you right. It just means that they are different from you. Simple as this may sound, it is a regular point of contention for most negotiators.

For instance, you may like to focus mainly on the pricing and contractual terms when involved in a business negotiation, but your counterpart may be more interested in the long-term relationship that might be established between you as individuals or between your respective organizations. It would not be accurate to think that, because it is a commercial transaction, only the money aspect is essential. Just because something is important and obvious to you does not mean that it is essential and obvious to someone else.

Your success as a negotiator will hinge first of all on your ability to honor your counterparts by recognizing and validating their preferences, especially when they differ from yours.

The power of understanding your negotiation preferences lies in the fact that self-awareness—and self-development—should strengthen your ability to adapt your negotiation stile in a way that will both honor and create a safe environment for your counterparts. It is this safe environment that persuades people to more readily share information and opportunity.

Confirmation Bias

A trend I see growing daily in both American and European cultures is that people tend to limit their sources of information to those that align with what they already believe: some people only accept stories from conservative news media groups, while others only accept news reports from left-leaning groups. Some call it "preaching to the choir," or "the echo-chamber." For our purposes here, we will refer to it as Confirmation Bias.

Confirmation Bias is the tendency for people to favor information that confirms their preconceptions or hypotheses, regardless of whether the information is accurate. As a result, people gather evidence and recall information from their memory selectively, and interpret it in a way that aligns exclusively with their predetermined understanding.

The biases manifest most prominently in emotionally-charged issues and among long-held beliefs. For example, in reading news about controversial issues like gun control or abortion, people prefer to read articles that align with and affirm their existing attitudes. They also tend to interpret ambiguous evidence as supporting their current position.

Biased search, interpretation, and recall have each been invoked to explain:

- **Attitude Polarization** (when a disagreement becomes divisive, even though both parties are exposed to the same evidence).

- **Belief Perseverance** (when beliefs persist after the evidence supporting them is shown to be false).

- **Irrational Primacy Effect** (when data encountered early in an arbitrary series is given preference or unjustified weight).

- **Illusory Correlation** (in which people falsely perceive an association between two events or situations).

A series of experiments in the 1960s by cognitive psychologist Peter Wason at University College in the United Kingdom demonstrated these forms of Confirmation Bias (of course, you can prove it yourself anecdotally by spending five minutes on social media). He demonstrated that people have a primal tendency to seek out information that proves what they already believe and filter out information that calls it into question. Later work explained these results in terms of a tendency to test ideas in a one-sided way, focusing on one possibility and ignoring alternatives. That will typically lead to outcomes that validate the bias—a "self-fulfilling prophecy."

When biases are identified and called out, they are sometimes explained as "wishful thinking" and "the limited human capacity to process information." Another theory is that people show confirmation bias because they are more interested in avoiding the psychological and emotional costs of being wrong than in investigating in a neutral, scientific way.

Confirmation biases contribute to overconfidence in personal beliefs and can maintain or strengthen beliefs in the face of contrary evidence, which can create an environment ripe for polarization. That can lead to disaster for relationships at every level, from corporations and governments to friendships and marriages.

Why all this talk about confirmation bias? To show that you and I will tend to prefer our own perceptions as we make decisions and prepare for our negotiations with our counterparts. The fact that we believe something to be true does not necessarily make it true. It is merely a perspective we hold, and therefore, subject to the limitations of our human reasoning. We should not close our minds and refuse to listen to those who may harbor perspectives different from ours. In fact, their view of the situation may be crucial to help us complete our own understanding. Letting go of personal perspectives is not something folks like to do. This limits opportunities and stunts personal growth.

A New Golden Rule

Having made the case that different things motivate people and that we all tend to be one-sided in justifying our own perspectives, how can we use this insight to lead to better deal-making?

Most of us have been raised by our parents to treat others as we wish to be treated. Some cultures refer to this as "the Golden Rule" and it is held up as the zenith of personal character. This is a noble goal and the intent behind it is admirable, but in the global, cross-cultural world we live in today, treating others the way we would like to be treated could seem a little presumptuous. What if their values run cross-wise of yours?

Let's consider a revised model: treating others the way they would like to be treated. It sounds simple—almost silly—but this simple adjustment will immediately improve the outcomes of your negotiations. The reason is straightforward: you will have to start asking your counterpart some questions. It is impossible to know how others would like to be treated without first asking questions. In addition, asking questions puts you in control of the conversation and positions you in your counterpart's mind as trustworthy, humble, and gracious. Our world trains us to position and persuade, instead of question, gather, and learn.

Over time, and having worked in 63 countries across the globe, I have come to realize that thinking of culture-defined behaviors in terms of right and wrong is not useful at all. In fact, it can be extremely counterproductive. Each human is an individual and even those sharing the same ethnic origin, culture, language, and skin tones will have a varying spectrum of beliefs and preferences, and this is a blessing. We judge and invalidate our counterparts' differences at our own peril.

How boring would life be if we all conformed to the same views, beliefs, and interests? One of the greatest perks of my line of work is the opportunity that I regularly get to meet people from all cultures, faiths, and walks of life. I find it fascinating that, while we can be drastically different in terms of our customs, habits, and behaviors, most often we desire similar things in life.

In my live workshops, I like to draw a chart like this to illustrate the point.

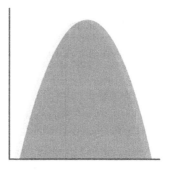

There are two groups represented here: the yellow group has one set of values and priorities, and the blue group has a different set of values and priorities. What is remarkable about these two groups is that they have over ninety percent of their values and priorities in common. In other words, what separates these two groups represents less than ten percent of their total values. I truly believe this is true of nearly all of our relationships. How foolish that we tend to focus on the tiny nuances that divide us. Perhaps it is a symptom of the polarized culture we see around us today, and perhaps it reflects something deeper in human nature: the need to be right.

The Big Mistake

Too often, when we enter into even the most ordinary negotiation, we expect our counterparts to share (and support) our views, beliefs, and interests. We believe that our proposal makes such obvious sense that, surely, they must see it the same way. When they don't, we decide it is a lack of insight or experience (or intelligence) on their part. We have the audacity to be surprised and offended.

This is, without a doubt, the single biggest mistake I see people make when they negotiate. It is arrogant to believe that because the argument seems so apparent to you, surely your counterpart will also agree to your logic...if only they would listen to you.

The Retail Problem

I recently visited London's Oxford Street shopping district just before Christmas. You probably know all too well what happens during the holiday shopping season—particularly in high-end stores: eager sales clerks slide up to you and ask, "Can I help you?" What do you do immediately, as if by reflex? If you're anything like me, you probably answer with something like, "No thank you, I'm just looking."

What do you naturally do when you perceive that someone is trying to sell you something? You instinctively move into a defensive posture. We don't enjoy being sold to, yet we like to purchase.

Think about this: when you are negotiating with somebody, your first inclination is to try to convince (sell) them on the validity of your idea based on your evidence and your perspective. But what do they naturally do? They defend their position—even if they might have otherwise agreed with what you have to say. The fact is you provoked the objection, just like the over-enthusiastic retail clerk.

Now let's turn the question around: do you enjoy buying things? I love shopping for electronics. I think it is a pretty universal constant of human nature that we enjoy buying things. Why, then, do we not like to be sold to? Why do we take a defensive posture when a salesperson is trying to sell us something that we want to buy? Why do people object to someone trying to move them toward an outcome we would otherwise desire?

To underline the point, a woman in one of my workshops recently told me this story:

"I went into [a big cellular company's] store because I wanted to buy my husband a phone for his fiftieth birthday. I went to the first sales guy I saw and said, 'I need to buy a cellphone. What phone should I get?' For the next fifteen minutes, he hammered me with all the features of one phone after another—signal coverage, apps, music, storage capacity, data plans. I didn't even know what he was talking about half the time. I was so overwhelmed. My head was swirling with information. I couldn't begin to make a decision. All I could say to him when he was done was, 'Thank you; I'll have to think about it.' I walked out of there as fast as I could, but I still had to buy a phone.

"I walked to the other end of the mall, into another cell phone store, hoping to get some better direction. I walked up to the middle-aged man behind the counter and said the same thing: 'I need to buy a cellphone. What phone should I get?' The salesman smiled and asked, "How will you be using this phone—for business or personal use?'

"I replied, 'I want to give it to my husband for his birthday.'

"'Listen,' he replied, 'if my wife bought me an iPhone X, I'd be so freaking happy.' Well, that was all I cared about. I went home with an iPhone X from that store."

What did the second sales clerk do right that the other did not? He didn't 'pitch' his prospect and he used the Rule of Reciprocity effectively.

The Rule of Reciprocity

The Rule of Reciprocity states that we return to others the form of behavior that they exhibit towards us. If I were to approach you in a contentious or combative manner, the Rule of Reciprocity would compel you to respond in kind—contentiously or combatively. Conversely, if I were to approach you with a view toward helping you achieve your desired outcome, then you are more likely to respond by helping me get what I want.

Sometimes we make life complicated for ourselves by provoking objections. Look at how the two sales clerks in the previous story used the Rule of Reciprocity:

The first sales clerk led with what was important to him—his knowledge of the technical specifications of the devices—which led to a confused customer leaving empty-handed.

The second clerk led with what the customer wanted—her desire to make her husband very happy on his birthday—and he got the sale.

If I were to approach you in a negotiation leading with a pile of facts and evidence that support my assumptions, and I don't consider your perspective at least as important, then I am setting myself up for an objection because you will feel the need to defend your beliefs. I'm not saying that you don't need facts and evidence to support your case; I am saying that when you lead with the evidence, you are more likely to provoke objections because reciprocity dictates that when you lead with your perspective, your counterpart naturally has to respond by positioning and/ or defending.

The challenge lies in breaking that reciprocity and recasting it. We will talk more about how to do that as we move through the rest of this book.

Simplify Your Life By Making Reciprocity Work For You

My life has become so much easier, both professionally and personally, since I realized that the easiest way to convince people to move in my direction is to advance in their direction first; to focus my energy on satisfying their unique and specific needs, rather than convincing them of the strength of my argument. The only way to uncover your counterpart's unique and particular perspective is by asking them questions.

Not only will you uncover information that is probably very relevant to your negotiation, but by demonstrating a genuine desire to support his needs and preferences, he will most likely be moved to be just as accommodating come time for your requests and needs. This is why the poker-faced, self-focused, clinical approach to negotiation seldom works: it restricts opportunities by aggravating relationships.

Stephen Covey said it best: "Seek first to understand, then to be understood."

Key Takeaways from Chapter Two

- Your negotiation capability is a function of three elements: your behavior, your competencies or skills, and your preferences.

- Your preferences drive your behavior more than your competencies ever will.

- Your preferences have been shaped by your psychological wiring.

- Brain research has shown that the four quadrants of the brain conduct different functions of thought and emotion, and all four work together for a "whole-brained" approach.

- Approximately three percent of all people have a preference for one quadrant at the exclusion of others; three percent have equal preference for all four quadrants; the remaining ninety four percent have a preference for either two or three quadrants.

- Preferences are unique to individuals, so it is inappropriate to designate another person's preferences as "right" or "wrong" when comparing them to your own.

- The four pillars of negotiation are Vision, Value, Relationship, and Process. You and your counterpart have preferences related to each of these pillars.

- Confirmation Bias is the tendency to accept only information that validates what you already believe.

- The Golden Rule states, "Do unto others as you would have done unto you," but this makes unwarranted assumptions about values and preferences. A more inclusive model is to "treat others the way they would like to be treated."

> *"If you come to a negotiation table saying you have the final truth, that you know nothing but the truth and that is final, you will get nothing."*
>
> —Harri Holkeri

Apply It To Your Situation

1. From your study of the Neethling Brain Instrument (NBI™), what quadrant(s) would you say are most comfortable to you? Which are the least comfortable?

_____

_____

_____

_____

2. Identify someone with whom you frequently interact. How would you characterize their NBI™ preferences? What insights do you gain from this about the nature of your interactions?

_____

_____

_____

_____

3. What are some confirmation biases that you harbor? Would you be willing to think differently about them, knowing how they could interfere with your negotiations?

_____

_____

_____

_____

4. If your preferences drive your behavior more than your competencies, what does that tell you about your ability to change long-established behaviors and habits in your life?

_____

_____

_____

Chapter Three: Identifying Interests

Executive Summary

- Fundamental to effective negotiation is understanding your counterpart's stated positions and the unstated interests behind them.

- Individuals have interests on different levels, as do organizations. Some will directly influence your negotiations, while others will not.

- To agree, often at least one party must change their position while at the same time still satisfying their interests. To protect the relationship, you must be prepared to allow your counterpart to "save face."

Preferences, Positions, and Interests

In the previous chapter, you discovered that different things motivate people. Now we will pause and look at the ways you can use this knowledge to help you close deals.

To understand interests accurately, we must first differentiate them from preferences and positions. Coming to the negotiation table, you have preferences, positions and interests, as does your counterpart:

- Your preferences can be defined as the way you like to do things, influenced by your values, beliefs, conditioning, and personality.

- A position is the declared stance that you or your counterparts have on any issue. In other words, this is usually the bit of information that we verbalize formally—"Our price is x" or "We need to buy twenty widgets."

- Interests are the drivers behind positions. In other words, an interest is the set of circumstances or objectives that support the declared position (e.g., "The reason our price is x is because we need to achieve a profit of y this quarter" or "The reason we need twenty widgets is because we have to keep up with the rapid growth in demand from our customers.")

It might seem like a fine semantic point, but the clearer you are on the differences between preferences, interests, and positions, the more effective you will be in any negotiation.

If you know the interests supporting your counterparts' positions, you can use some creativity to find multiple ways to satisfy what they really want. Not being aware of this difference can severely restrict your ability to reach even the most basic agreement. So how can we uncover the unspoken interests behind our counterparts' positions? Uncovering interests is best achieved by using a questioning approach and through being diligent in your preparations before negotiations commence.

Recognizing The Real Motivation Behind The Request

Let's take an example from marriage. I remember a time my wife asked me to go shopping with her. It caught my attention because it was not something she normally asked me to do. She likes shopping alone. My first instinct was to say "no" because shopping with her held no interest for me.

My Position: My position was that I wanted to play golf during that time.

My Interests: My interests were that golf helped me relax and I enjoyed time with my golfing buddies.

At that moment, Linda's position conflicted with my position, and a negotiation was about to take place. It could turn out well for both of us (we call that "win/win"), turn out badly for both of us ("lose/lose"), or one could win at the other's expense ("win/lose").

But then another thought crossed my mind: having me go shopping with her was her stated position, but what was the driver or interest behind that position? I am not always the most attentive husband in the world, and it seemed that she wanted me to validate the importance of our relationship by spending time with her doing things she enjoys. Is that the kind of thing most people come right out and say? Probably not. She may not even have been consciously aware of that interest; she just knew that it was essential to her that I went with her that time.

We each had a choice to make at that moment—am I willing to take the first step toward an agreement? Later in the book we will talk about moving toward a desirable middle ground through making concessions, but for now let's just say I got a really nice new shirt out of the deal and quality time with my wife, doing something neither of us typically enjoys doing with others. There was an atypical interest behind her request that I uncovered simply by wanting to understand what was motivating her request.

The Key To "Win/Win" Scenarios

One meaningful way we can improve the odds that we will enjoy a "win/win" scenario in almost any negotiation is by seeking out and accurately addressing each other's interests. If you can understand the interests of all the parties involved in your negotiation, you can uncover common ground and open up opportunities for you to creatively address those positions.

Successful negotiators at home and in the marketplace look past the stated position to identify the unstated interests: why does she want me to go shopping with her and what need does it fulfill?

In doing so, you are more likely to find that you and your counterpart have interests in common and adjust your position to align with theirs. We'll talk more about finding common interests in a moment.

Pinpointing Interests

While the positions people may take in any given situation are unique to that situation, some of the interests that motivate them are common to all people in one form or another. Psychologist Abraham Maslow identified five (and later eight[1]) major categories of needs that all humans experience. He organized them into a hierarchy ranging from creature comforts to self- actualization in his 1943 paper, "A Theory of Human Motivation."[2] This is also referred to as "Maslow's Hierarchy."

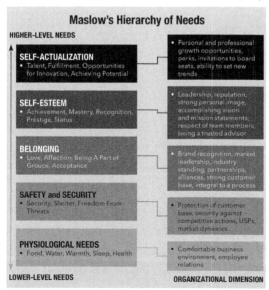

---

1   Maslow, A., (1971). The farther reaches of human nature. New York: The Viking Press
2   Maslow, A., (1943). A theory of human motivation. Psychological Review, 50, 370-396

Knowing that a limited palette of interests drives all behaviors and positions makes it easier to respond appropriately to the interests behind your counterpart's positions, whether they can verbalize them or not. I believe you will find that, when you can connect your position to a specific interest your counterpart holds, the outcomes will be more satisfying to all parties.

Let's say I wanted to buy my children a puppy. I visit a local breeder selling puppies, but the price he is asking is more than I want to spend. With a little questioning, I might learn that the breeder has a strong interest that the puppies go to good families and that the homes have fenced yards with plenty of room to run. If I know I meet those qualifications, I can use that information to help me negotiate a lower price. It's that simple; by focusing on his (usually silent) interest—the driver behind his position—I get a better deal.

Business Interests

Fortunately, basic human needs are easy to identify: food, water, shelter, clothing, love, affection, community, fulfillment, and so on. But what do needs look like in the work environment? Here are some examples:

Sample Personal Interests In A Work Environment:

- Promotion
- Recognition
- More family time
- Reduced conflict
- Increased power/Influence
- Improves social status
- Autonomy
- Job security
- Self-esteem
- Financial well-being
- Security/safety
- Leadership development
- Team morale
- Inspiration/motivation
- Education

Note that there are typically multiple sets of interests that play a role when you negotiate. Even in a simple negotiation, each person at the table will have both personal and business interests, and both types of interests will play a role in how the negotiation plays out.

Personal interests really could be just about anything. They will often relate to the person's work role/position/satisfaction, but they may well also be based on something entirely outside of the work sphere.

What's more, your counterpart's personal interests and business interests may even be at odds. I may have a business interest in raising my sales numbers which may require more time at work and a personal interest in having more family time. Those interests are, at least on the surface, at odds.

Identifying Your Counterparts' Interests

As you think about your counterpart's interests, it is helpful to ask them questions in a variety of categories:

- **Personal Interests**—these may include such basic human needs as security, economic well-being, recognition, or control over one's life.

- **Business Interests**—these might include reduced costs/expenditures, increasing profits, or long-term strategic fit.

- **Long-term/Short-term Interests**—these can be as different as market leadership vs. daily cash flow.

- **Intangible Interests**—these are the benefits we want to gain or the costs we want to avoid, such as money and financial security, relationships, reputation, and face-saving.

One of the most important questions you should develop the habit of asking yourself is: "If I were in my counterpart's shoes, what would I care or worry about?" Then develop some questions to verify your assumptions. Be sure to plan on also asking why those things are important to them. We call these probing and nurturing questions that uncover interests.

Remember that, while positions are concrete and explicit, interests are often intangible, sometimes counter-intuitive, and even inconsistent. For example, in a job interview, someone who is outwardly driving for more money may internally be seeking out recognition. If they feel that money is a means of gaining recognition for their expertise, then a small raise—along with a focused effort to make them feel appreciated and needed—may very well satisfy their unspoken needs.

Organizations Have Needs, Too

Organizations also have interests, some of which are similar to individual interests. You will find that when you negotiate in a business context, each of the stakeholders often will be representing not only their personal interests but also the interests of their organization. Consider these organizational interests and question who in the organization might best represent these interests:

- Sample Organizational Interests
- Raising revenues
- ROI/ROA—Profitability
- Increasing market share
- Getting higher dividends
- Lowering expenses
- Low cost of ownership
- Good budget fit
- Increased productivity
- Risk management
- Cash flow management
- Customer loyalty
- Product/solution specifications
- Best technical solution
- Best value for the money
- Long-term strategic fit
- Increasing efficiency
- Price performance
- Protecting the client base
- Competitive advantage
- Increased sales
- Market reach
- Reduced cost of sales/ purchasing

Buying Roles Within Organizations And Their Respective Interests

In their landmark book, **Strategic Selling**, Robert Miller and Stephen Heiman identified three distinct buyer types that operate in most organizations, no matter the size or structure. Their terminology has become established as part of the standard vocabulary in the corporate sales environment.

The reason it is crucial to understand the different types of buyer is that each type influences the buying decision in a specific way, because each is interested in different aspects of the sales proposition:

1. Economic Buyer (Approver/Decision Maker): approves the decision and releases the money (e.g., CEO, CFO, Marketing Director, Training Director). This person is typically interested in:

   - Exceeding their goals at any price

   - ROI

   - Increasing benefits, market share, etc.

   - Raising revenues

   - Increasing efficiency

   - Attracting new customers and repeating customers

   - Increasing dividends

   - Stakeholder management

   - Getting products to market quicker than the competition

   - Decreasing the downtime of revenue-producing employees

   - Lowering the cost of sales

   - Reducing expenses

   - Increased sales

   - Reduced cost of sales

2. Technical Buyer: influences the decision to purchase your product or service (e.g., Procurement Manager, IT Manager/Director). This person is typically interested in:

   - A product that meets high specifications

   - Timely delivery

   - Best technical solution

- The latest and most excellent product / service

- Accumulation of knowledge power

- Little or no risk

- The most correct, zero-defect solution possible

- Getting the best performance for the price

- Recognition as the ultimate problem-solver

- Total cost of ownership

- Reducing expenses

3. User Buyer: may recommend your product or service to his/her organization (e.g., line manager, business unit manager, an individual user of your product or service). You want to make this person's job easier in any way you can. They are typically interested in:

- Increased efficiency

- Increased productivity

- Reliability

- Team performance enhancement

- Fulfills performance promise

- Best problem-solver

- Does the job better / faster / easier

- Super-service / User-friendly

Asking Questions To Identify Interests

The key to accurately addressing the interests behind your counterparts' positions is getting your counterparts to verbalize them by asking questions. It could be as simple as asking why they hold a specific position.

Example 1:

Position: "We will only do business with American organizations."

You ask: "Do you mind if I ask why you have this stipulation?"

Interest: "We have encountered delays and frustrations enforcing agreed-to guidelines with companies outside of the United States."

Example 2:

Position: "I want to buy a watch for my husband."

You ask: "May I ask why you are in the market for this gift?"

Interest: "My son accidentally broke the watch, and I don't want my husband to find out and become angry, so I want an identical replacement as soon as possible."

Key Takeaways

You will recognize from these examples that understanding the interest behind the position provides you with critical information that should direct the rest of your conversation. Uncovering the interest behind the desire shown in the watch replacement example will give you an idea of how much the customer might be willing to spend on the item.

In some circumstances, it may take more than one "why" question to uncover a deeper set of interests. In the case of the company that would only do business with American organizations, the deeper issue might be rooted in one person's mistrust of foreigners that became a corporate policy. A follow-up question might be, "Can you give me an example of a situation where this problem arose?"

You may find out through a series of questions that the company no longer employs the person who initiated the policy, and their successor is willing to reconsider working with vendors from outside the country.

More People, More Complexity

As you can imagine, the more parties involved in the negotiation, the more complicated this landscape becomes. For example, one of the frequent complaints I hear from professional purchasing organizations is that, while negotiating with vendors can be relatively easy (aside from single source and sole vendors), trying to get internal agreement about exactly what to buy and what can be spent is often the greater challenge. Internal negotiations consistently rank highest on the list of challenges and frustrations in negotiation.

When agents or mediators are brought in, it adds layers of complexity. The agent not only needs to represent your businesses interests but they also need to satisfy their own personal interests and the interests of their company.

Here is a list of questions you can use to help you uncover your counterpart's interests:

- What are your long-term objectives for the business?

- What are your short- or medium-term objectives?

- What are you aiming to get from this deal?

- What will happen if you don't solve this problem or overcome your challenges with_____?

- To make sure that we can offer a solution that meets your requirements, please help me understand_____.

- What is the number one priority for you?

- Why is it important?

- As I understand it, your interests are_____.

- May I ask why?

- Is there a reason why you are not pursuing another option?

- What are the top three critical elements of the deal you are looking for?

- How will you measure success?

- Who are the key stakeholders?

- In addition to you, who else will be involved in decision making?

- What is the main thing you are trying to accomplish this year?

- What is your primary concern about_____?

- What are the specific goals for your organization over the next month/quarter/year?

- What are your criteria for establishing a business relationship?

- What is the crucial deal maker/breaker for your team regarding this project?

- How long have you had this need?

Don't Overlook the Basics

In searching for the interests behind a declared position, start by looking for those bedrock concerns which motivate all people. If you can take care of such basic needs, you increase the chance both of reaching an agreement and, if an agreement is reached, of the other side honoring it. As we observed before, the most basic human needs include:

- Security

- Economic well-being

- A sense of belonging

- Recognition

- Control over one's life

As fundamental as they are, basic human needs are easy to overlook, so it bears repeating here. It is easy to get lured into thinking that the only interest people and organizations have is money. This Is often the position communicated, but it is rarely the silent driver—the interest—behind the decision making process.

A Simple Way To Think About Interests

All interests boil down to either the desire to change something or the desire to keep things the way they are. Understanding this allows you to put your counterpart's interests into a context where you can effectively align your propositions and suggestions to their needs.

The quadrants below are a helpful framework for identifying and prioritizing your counterparts' interests (as well as your own):

	Have	**Don't Have**	
	Keep / Maintain / Improve	Obtain / Develop / Build	**Want**
	Eliminate / Fix / Solve	Avoid / Prevent	**Don't Want**

Questions To Identify Interests

- What do you or your counterpart already have and want? These are the things that you or your counterpart would like to keep, maintain, or improve.

- What do you or your counterpart not have that you want? These are the things that you would like to obtain, build, or develop.

- What are the things that you and your counterpart don't want, but have? These are the interests that you wish to eliminate, fix, or solve.

- What are the things that you and your counterpart don't have and don't want? These are the things that you want to avoid or prevent.

The Need To Be Right (Saving Face)

There is a human interest that represents one of the most significant differences between Eastern and Western cultures. When I consult or train in the Middle East or the Far East, I can spend about fifteen minutes on this topic and move on. But when I coach in the United States, Canada, or Europe, it seems like I can spend an hour on this topic and it still doesn't really take hold in my clients' minds. I am speaking of the principle of allowing your counterpart to "save face."

When negotiators bargain over positions, they tend to lock themselves into those positions, especially if there is significant financial or emotional weight behind them. When a negotiation reaches an impasse, most people tend to clarify and defend their own position—to "dig in their heels" and try to force their counterpart to concede. The more you try convincing the other side to change their position, the more difficult your task will become. This is a low level of negotiation skill.

The first party to change their position runs the risk of being humiliated or taken advantage of by their counterparts. Consider the political climates in the United States and the European Union. Emotions will often run high on both sides of each argument put forward by a political party, and the harder one side fights to impose their will, the more the other side entrenches their own view.

However, arguing over positions prevents the parties from forming and maintaining mutually beneficial relationships, which is the ultimate desired outcome of most negotiations. If both parties feel at risk of being shamed, they are less likely to extend trust and goodwill across the table. This is where my colleagues in the East have a significant strategic advantage over the West: they give each other room to "save face," or to modify their firmly-held positions with dignity and flexibility. Westerners would benefit significantly from embracing this skill.

What we don't realize is that it is doubtful that your counterpart will move in your direction if you have not created any room for him to move safely in your direction. In your pursuit of convincing him that your perspective is the correct one, you may well have made it impossible for him to move in your direction without sacrificing his credibility. When faced with sacrificing his credibility, it is much more likely that he will refuse to advance in your direction, even if he knows that your suggestion is the best course of action. In other words, he is likely to forego the benefits of moving in your direction because it is more critical to maintain his dignity than to participate in the benefits you are presenting.

Rather than put him in that losing position, make room for him to "save face." How that manifests will be unique to each negotiation, but it ultimately comes down to making room for him to adjust his position without it looking like he is surrendering or caving in. The experienced, confident negotiator seeks to help his counterpart to succeed. This characteristic can alter the course of all your future negotiations.

Key Takeaways from Chapter Three

- Positions are explicitly stated stances each party takes on any issue. Interests are the drivers behind positions, including circumstances, objectives, emotions, and preconceptions.

- Interests are often unexpressed, intangible, and may be inconsistent. Individuals have personal interests and business interests. These may be aligned or in conflict with one another, but they all drive behavior.

- It is critical to understand the interests behind the positions of all parties in your negotiations.

- Interests may be ascertained by asking questions.

- All humans have basic needs that fall along a hierarchy illustrated by Dr Abraham Maslow.

- Organizations have interests that are represented by various stakeholders.

- The more stakeholders are involved in a negotiation, the more complex the interests become.

- People have a legitimate need to be right, even when changing an established position. To protect relationships and create space to move in your direction, it is critical to give your counterpart room to "save face" and maintain their dignity during negotiation.

> *"Any fool can criticize, condemn, and complain but it takes character and self-control to be understanding and forgiving."*

> — Dale Carnegie

Apply It To Your Situation

1. Think about a negotiation you are likely to face. What are your positions in that negotiation? What are your counterpart's positions? What interests are driving your positions? What interests do you believe might be driving your counterpart's position?

   _____

   _____

   _____

   _____

2. What questions could you ask to verify your assumptions about your counterpart's interests?

   _____

   _____

   _____

   _____

3. Who are the other stakeholders in the negotiation? What is likely to be their interests in this negotiation? How might you address those interests?

   _____

   _____

   _____

   _____

Chapter Four: Negotiation Strategy

Executive Summary

- To move to the next level of negotiation competence, it is essential that you move from negotiating by default to negotiating by design.

- There are five fundamental negotiation strategies. Compete, Compromise, Avoid, Accommodate, and Collaborate.

- You are likely to have a default strategy that you prefer to use, but you will maximize your results by learning how to deploy all five with equal ability.

- Your negotiation style preference profile is an indication of your default approach to negotiations.

- A Collaborative approach to negotiation is not necessarily the correct approach.

Let's Go Back To The Golf Course

I want to start this chapter on strategy by returning to our golf analogy.

A typical golfer's bag contains fourteen clubs, including a putter, a driver, a set of irons, woods, and wedges. As a golfer, your job is to select the right tool for the challenge at hand and use it appropriately. You would never approach golf in a "linear" fashion, as we described earlier (e.g., "I always hit the driver, followed by the three wood, then the two iron, then the three iron, etc.") That would be crazy. Why? Because all golfers know better than to reduce their golf game to a pattern of using the same combination of clubs in the same order for every situation.

Of course, every golfer has a favorite club, and they look for every opportunity to use it. But golfers who want to advance their game learn to hit all their clubs and adapt their club choice to the unique requirements of each hole and each game.

Smart golfers (and smart negotiators):

- Identify the goal

- Recognize the current conditions and parameters

- Select the right tool to accomplish the objective in each unique circumstance

Whether or not we are conscious of it, each of us has formed habits and preferences in the way we approach negotiation—whether it's with your spouse, your boss, or a customer. We tend to approach every negotiation with a similar mindset and thought process. Often, that favorite approach gets the desired result, but sometimes it doesn't. Your default approach has gotten you to where you are today, but to go to the next level and achieve better results, you will have to move past your default practices and bring intentional design to every negotiation. It will be uncomfortable at first as you practice unfamiliar skills, but over time, you will come to enjoy the freedom and flexibility your wider skillset will afford you.

If we were studying golf, we would want to move you away from swinging a seven-iron at everything, and give you a wider 'vocabulary' of clubs and strokes. We would broaden your game plan to address changes in the weather, the wind, the dampness of the grass, stiffness in the shoulders, time constraints, and your current position relative to the pin. You could find yourself in the exact same place on the exact same fairway you were on yesterday, but with a heightened awareness of the current conditions, you will have the ability to play it differently than you did yesterday and get a better result.

In golf and negotiation, you want to make sure that the strategy, tactics, tools, and techniques you select matches the unique demands of the situation at hand, even if everything about the situation looks the same as it always has. Let's take a look at five different negotiation strategies you can apply.

Winning And Losing

Academics typically characterize negotiations in terms of "winning" and "losing." As a result of literature that has been published by some of the world's leading academics over the past few decades, the "win/win situation" is such a common desired outcome that it has become a part of our vernacular. You most likely have heard people around you looking for a "win/win" in situations where two parties' objectives would otherwise seem to be at odds.

But when understanding negotiation in a real-world context, the "win/lose" concept is inadequate. While "win/win" sounds good, both parties getting exactly what they want is not always desirable, especially if your counterpart's goal would be detrimental to your well-being (e.g., their intent may be to shut down your company). At the same time, "lose/lose" sounds like a total failure, but in some circumstances, may be precisely what both parties need at the moment.

There will be times when you will need to transition from one strategy to another during a negotiation. To return to our golf analogy, the "win/lose" construct is like trying to play all eighteen holes with a driver and a seven iron. Successful negotiation requires us to be as flexible as possible to get the best outcome in any situation.

Viewing Strategy From Two Dimensions

When considering your negotiation strategy, it is useful to think of two dimensions first codified by Kenneth W. Thomas and Ralph H. Kilmann and deployed in their Thomas-Kilmann Conflict Mode Instrument (TKI):

1. The satisfaction of your counterpart's goals, objectives, and interests (or your level of cooperativeness).

2. The achievement of your own goals, objectives, and interests (or your level of assertiveness).

According to Kenneth W. Thomas and Ralph H. Kilmann, the five conflict management modes (or in our case, negotiation strategies), are made up of different balances of these two dimensions—assertiveness and cooperativeness, spread along two axes, as expressed in this graphic:

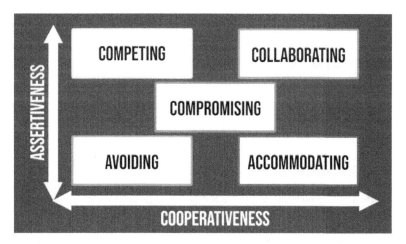

This graphic shows how each of the five fundamental strategies considers both dimensions:

AVOIDING

When you are unassertive and uncooperative, you avoid negotiating. This is typically referred to as a "lose/lose" scenario, but you can probably think of times when the best thing for both parties to do is walk away. An avoiding strategy is commonly deployed for commoditized, relatively low value, non- strategic online bids or e-bids as a first step to inviting and selecting potential vendors.

COMPETING

When you are assertive and uncooperative, you are being competitive. If you are buying office supplies and ten different vendors are bidding, you may not need to be cooperative in the same way you would if there were only one. This type of approach is typically referred to as "win/lose" type negotiations. Again, it's worth asking if your counterpart is really losing every time you are assertive, or if it should matter to you.

ACCOMMODATING

When you are cooperative and unassertive, you are accommodating. This is typically referred to as "lose/win" type negotiations or "taking one for the team." You may decide that, to protect the long-term relationship with your counterpart, it's worth making a concession this time. If you are launching a new and unproven product, you might want to offer it to your clients at a steep discount until you have a chance to establish the value of it. Accommodating can be a very smart, strategic first step in high-stake, strategic negotiations.

COMPROMISING

When you are somewhat cooperative and somewhat assertive, then you meet in the middle, and you are said to compromise. This is typically referred to as a "win/win" scenario. Nobody gets everything they want, but everybody gets something. We take the proverbial pie and split it between us.

COLLABORATING

When you are both highly assertive and highly cooperative, you are collaborating. The academic world considers this approach to be the "holy grail" of negotiation. It is often known as a "win more/win more" negotiation, where you create truly synergistic agreements and partnerships. You get everything you want and give your counterpart everything they want. It's not just that everyone gets a piece of the pie; instead, everyone gets a pie. It sounds Utopian, and it is often described in such lofty terms, but as you will see later in this chapter, it's not always the right thing to do.

I'm going to spend the balance of this chapter dissecting and analyzing these five strategies, so you can identify situations where each would be useful in your negotiations. While it would be tempting to assume that one of these strategies is always the best option for you, I hope that you will recognize the value of adding all five to your toolkit.

The Logistics of A Negotiation

Let's move this discussion into more of a real-world scenario to consider how these different strategies might come into play. Take a moment and imagine you are the purchasing agent representing a logistics solution provider, such as FedEx or DHL. Let's say you are assigned to buy a variety of products and solutions, for instance, a new fleet of trucks, stationery for the office, fuel, and enterprise resource planning software. You are going to need to meet with a wide range of vendors, each with strengths, weaknesses, needs, and interests.

1. Purchasing New Trucks

Let's consider how you might go about buying new vehicles. Do you think that it would make a strategic difference to FedEx whether they purchased a range of Mercedes trucks or a range of Ford trucks? While the truck manufacturers will most certainly put across a strong case as to why their vehicles would provide an important strategic advantage over their competitors, the truth of the matter is that it is unlikely that the choice of the truck manufacturer will have a significant strategic impact on FedEx.

When buying something that you believe is expensive in terms of cost but not likely to deliver substantial strategic impact to the organization, you would most likely pursue a competitive negotiation strategy where you are not as concerned about the relationship dynamics. Typically, in this situation, you would probably put in place an RFP (Request for Proposal) process, identify a shortlist of two or three providers, and then effectively play them off against each other to obtain the best possible offer based on price. You are in a position of relative power in that they have to win your business and you get to set the terms.

2. Purchasing Stationery

In the case of purchasing stationery, what strategy should you pursue? It is unlikely to have a strategic impact on your organization if you were to run out (you would be able to get more stationery relatively easily). In this case, it may be worthwhile to consider avoiding negotiation altogether. Many large enterprises today are using online e-procurement systems with an auction capability to conduct these types of negotiations.

You could just set up an e-auction and award the business to the lowest bidder—no negotiation required. In situations like this, where it is not strategically critical to maintain relationships with commodity vendors, avoiding negotiation will allow you to focus more time, money, and resources on negotiations where the relationships are more strategic to the business.

3. Purchasing Fuel

Without fuel, your logistics company would find it difficult to survive; after all, your business is all about moving things around, usually with vehicles. A wise strategy in this category would include more than one supplier, creating redundancy to ensure a consistent supply in the event one vendor would default. Even though your spend on fuel might be a significant amount, it would still be regarded as an operational expense rather than a capital expense, so your strategy will need to consider that.

Your negotiation strategy in this scenario is likely to include more compromising and will focus more on relationship dynamics than in the previous two cases. You will likely need to provide your suppliers with some insight into your supply chain. This insight will give them the ability to adjust to your increasing needs intelligently as you expand and grow. For instance, if you were to open new locations or add to your fleet, you would need to notify them of these events to ensure that they can supply you at the locations and volumes required. Because the relationship is strategically important to you, the vendor in this scenario has considerably more power in the negotiation than the truck vendor and the stationery vendor, and you will need to be more accommodating.

4.   Purchasing Enterprise Resource Planning (ERP) Software

The purchase of an ERP (Enterprise Resource Planning) software system, such as Oracle ERP or SAP, is a significant investment for any company. It is often a multi-million-dollar transaction resulting in a business relationship that will remain in place for at least ten years. While you may start negotiations with potential suppliers with a competitive strategy, once you've selected a supplier, the relationship becomes all-important. You would expect your partner to understand your business deeply so they can assist you in the achievement of your strategic corporate objectives, so you would endeavor to follow a collaborative negotiation strategy.

As you can see, there is value to pursuing different negotiation strategies based on the merits of the kind of deal you wish to reach. You wouldn't want to spend the same amount of time, money, and resources building a relationship with a stationery vendor as you would with a custom software developer. Time, money, and resources are finite, so you have to discriminate in your use of these strategies to ensure that you achieve an optimal rate of return on your negotiation efforts.

Now let's see how you can apply these strategies to your negotiations.

Applying the Five Fundamental Negotiation Strategies

Competitive Strategy

It is appropriate to take a competitive (assertive) stance in your negotiations when any of these apply:

- The relationship is unimportant to you.

- You're buying a product or solution that is a commodity you can easily replace or source elsewhere.

- You must take quick action, and there is no time to debate the issues, as in an emergency.

- You must take a difficult or unpopular course of action, such as implementing a freeze on salary increases.

An assertive and uncooperative mode is power-oriented. When competing, you pursue only your concerns and objectives, possibly at your counterpart's expense, using whatever power seems appropriate to get your way (but always treating your counterparts with dignity, honor, and respect). Competing might mean standing up for your rights, defending a position you believe is correct, or simply trying to win your desired outcome.

Some of your counterparts will have strategic value to your organization in terms of prestige, referrals, or the ability to engage in multiple levels of collaboration. At the same time, some do not, and it is vital to recognize the difference, particularly where you have lots of alternatives available. Sometimes, you should simply set the terms of the relationship and move forward with whoever is willing to accept those terms.

While it is tempting to want to wield power every time you come to the negotiating table, it is important to realize that a competitive strategy is not always the best way to approach negotiations. Sometimes, you do not hold all the winning cards. While there may be short-term value to taking an assertive approach in many situations, it can hinder your ability to cultivate long-term relationships, and it's easy to burn bridges. There are a few business models where one-off transactions are a sustainable model, but most organizations do best when they can perpetuate repeat customers and long-term suppliers.

This is as true in the nonprofit and government sectors as it is in the business world. In fact, it is true in any interaction between humans. People and organizations who consistently assert their own goals and preferences over their counterparts' will eventually run out of new people who are willing to talk with them. Think of a family member or co-worker who always demands their way; do you always give them what they want or do you eventually look for ways to avoid them?

If you default to a competitive style, always focused only on your objectives, then I challenge you to make a concerted effort to ask questions of your counterpart to understand her interests and aspirations. In many cases, you will identify other opportunities to work together toward mutually beneficial ends. In almost all cases, you will foster a more enjoyable, longer-lasting working relationship.

Now, that is not to suggest that you never stand your ground, particularly if you're negotiating about something that's important to you or your organization. There are times when you must set the terms of engagement and act decisively. The critical thing is to discern when it is appropriate to do so.

Avoiding

It is appropriate to avoid negotiations when any of these apply:

- The relationship is unimportant.

- An issue is trivial, and it makes sense to stay out of it.

- The risks of engaging in a negotiation outweigh the benefits.

- You can use an "auction" process instead of face-to-face negotiation.

- You need to delay deciding or taking action until you have more information.

Again, we are discussing a scenario where your counterpart has little or no strategic value to your organization; you can take them or leave them. There will always be someone else to fill that spot. Remember, of course, the warning from the competitive approach not to be too fickle with people who could have long-term value to you.

If you have a high preference for avoiding, then it is incumbent upon you to get into the practice of engaging with your counterparts, if for no other reason than to uncover common ground. It's imperative to understand your counterparts' objectives and priorities because we tend to assign different values to different items. It may be that something you regard as insignificant is viewed as critical by your counterpart. You could be leaving money on the table if you don't take the time to investigate their needs.

If you have a low preference for avoiding—you feel like you need to get involved in everything—you should be aware that not all issues that you come across require you to engage. You absolutely should avoid some negotiations, especially if the potential risks outweigh the potential benefits.

Accommodating

It is appropriate to take an accommodating stance in your negotiations when any of these apply:

- The relationship with your counterpart is essential to you.

- The product or solution is strategic to you and your organization.

- Your offering is new or unproven in the market.

- Your counterpart has many high-quality alternatives available to them.

- The issue at hand is more important to the other person than it is to you, and you have an opportunity to create goodwill and foster the relationship.

An accommodating approach is both cooperative and unassertive—the opposite of competitive negotiation. When accommodating, you set aside your concerns and objectives to satisfy the interests and goals of your counterpart; there is an element of self-sacrifice in this mode.

I recently interviewed a talented young man to join my team. It was evident from the get-go that this job was important to him and to his family's well-being and that he was accustomed to bending over backward to accommodate people. He came with a long list of everything he could do for the company but didn't state a salary requirement. When I asked about it, he said, "whatever you think it's worth." He assumed that I had several other, more qualified candidates to choose from, and he wanted to create goodwill upfront. This meeting might be an extreme case, but it illustrates the point.

I offered him a compensation package that I knew was over and above what he would have asked. I wish I had a picture of the look on his face to show you. The fact was I knew that he was talented enough to find work elsewhere at a good salary, and I wanted to create some goodwill of my own. We have enjoyed working together ever since. He has since learned to say no to new projects when he feels overwhelmed, and I have been mindful not to overload him.

With a competitive approach, I could have taken advantage of his unassertive style and paid him as little as I could legally get away with, and I know several business owners who would have done just that. In the short term, that might have been advantageous to me, but it would not have fostered a long, positive working relationship, which is what my company needs. He would have come to resent me over time and, to the extent that his self-confidence would allow, would have sought better terms elsewhere.

If you have a high preference for accommodation, you should realize that, while it may not be natural or comfortable to you, it is often vital to stand firm on issues that are strategic or critical to you. Negotiation should be characterized as a mutually beneficial exchange on some level, not martyrdom.

Over the past seventeen years, I've encountered thousands of negotiators with an accommodating preference, and I've learned that an overly accommodating preference can be as destructive to relationships as an excessively competitive preference. Often the person with the accommodating preference reaches a stage where they feel like they are always the one making the concessions, keeping their counterparts happy at all cost while their own needs are overlooked or ignored. They seldom, if ever, declare their needs and interests and so they have significant unmet expectations of which their counterparts were not even aware. That leads to resentment, which can simmer for years until it finally explodes in an outburst that surprises everyone involved. Then the relationship is tarnished, if not ended entirely, and it all could have been avoided if both parties had taken the time to ask good questions and openly express real needs. If this is you, make sure that you share what your fundamental interests and goals are with your counterparts, as they will be unable to serve your interests if they don't know what they are.

If, on the other hand, you have a low preference for accommodation, you should focus on asking questions to understand your counterpart's perspective. Also, be aware that not all your objectives are critical; it may be possible for you to be accommodating on some objectives if this would ultimately advance the negotiation. The key is not to do the wrong thing for selfish reasons.

Compromising

Compromise is one of those words that has taken on a variety of connotations, both positive and negative, over recent years. Intermediate in both assertiveness and cooperativeness, the objective of compromise is to find an expedient, mutually acceptable solution that satisfies both parties, at least partially. Compromising falls on the middle ground between competing and accommodating, with each party giving up more than they would if they were competing but less than they would if they were accommodating. Compromising might mean splitting the difference, exchanging concessions, or seeking a quick middle ground position.

It is appropriate to compromise in your negotiations when any of these apply:

- The relationship and substantive goals are moderately important.

- The product or solution is moderately strategic to you and your organization.

- There is potential for growth and increased common ground in the future.

- Both you and your counterpart have some good quality alternatives available.

Depending on your point of view, it is important to realize that compromise is not always the right thing to do, nor is it consistently the wrong thing to do. The value of a compromise is affected by many factors, much like your golf game, so it requires careful preparation and evaluation.

If you have a high preference for compromising, you should know it may not always be necessary for you to engage in negotiation at all. It may also be useful for you to realize that you shouldn't always settle for the obvious, quick deal; if time allows, you should explore the options in more detail to move your deals onto a collaborative platform.

If you have a low preference for compromising, you should consider being more willing to find the middle ground and advance the relationship by settling on a solution that goes part-way toward addressing both your and your counterpart's objectives. This is especially true if you tend to be competitive. If you tend to be more accommodating, the opposite is true: a compromising approach will require you to be willing to give up less and ask for more.

Collaborating

Collaborating certainly sounds like the pinnacle outcome for any negotiation, and in a theoretical sense at least, that may be true. But in the real world, there are several factors to consider when seeking out a collaborative engagement. Both assertive and cooperative, collaboration is the opposite of avoiding, so there is no room for passivity. When collaborating, you attempt to work with your counterpart to find a solution that fully satisfies both your and your counterpart's concerns and objectives, and then goes beyond it all to build something greater. Instead of splitting the proverbial pie, you find or create additional pies so that you each end up with at least a pie. So, the result is synergistic: the total is more than the sum of the parts.

When we think about conflict resolution or international treaties, a collaborative approach must be the aim. But from a business perspective, how many deals you have seen in the genuinely collaborative space? Hardly any, right? Yet, that's always the aspiration.

Collaboration may be appropriate when any of these apply:

- Both the substantive, tangible goals and the relationship are essential to you and your organization.

- The product or solution is strategic to you and your organization.

- You have few or no high-quality alternatives available should negotiations fail.

- You want to draw from your counterpart's perspective to find an innovative solution to a complex problem.

- By merging perspectives, you draw from a broader range of expertise and experience.

If you have a high preference for collaboration, you should be aware that not all negotiations are strategic. You should carefully assess at what level you should commit to negotiations, or you are likely to overinvest in your negotiation exchanges. It is not necessary to develop deep, long-term relationships with counterparts in categories that don't hold the promise of strategic impact, although you must always treat your counterpart with dignity, honor, and respect.

If you have a low preference for collaboration, consider that in strategic negotiations, there should be a focus on the interests of all parties to optimize the negotiated outcomes. You'll often be able to achieve your own goals by assisting others in realizing theirs.

What Words Mean

When looking at these five fundamental negotiation strategies, it strikes me that there is a difference in how most people understand these words and their meaning versus their real meaning. And that's not an English language issue alone; it's the same thing in German, French, and other languages.

Often, when we say "collaborate," what we mean is "accommodate." We are picking up on the cooperative aspect of collaboration, which is only half of the equation. If you ask most people if collaboration means being assertive, they will say no. In reality, being collaborative is as much an assertive mode of negotiation as it is cooperative. This is a departure from the classic "win/lose" mentality because it's not just that only you or only your counterpart wins, but indeed both parties gain from being both cooperative and assertive in equal measure.

Another word that confuses people is the word "assertive." I have mentioned this several times already, but I think it bears repeating: it is a matter of personal character to treat your counterpart with dignity and respect at all times, even with the people who sell you a commodity as strategically unimportant as stationery. Being in an assertive, powerful posture doesn't mean that you don't have to treat people with dignity and respect.

You can be very assertive and still be nice—the two concepts are not mutually exclusive. You might say, "Listen, I would love for us to be able to work together, but it's just not going to be possible under these terms. But if anything changes, I stand ready to do work with you." I think we have in our collective mind a vision of assertive people being pushy jerks, treating people rudely or impolitely, and not respecting their needs. That need not be the case. The ability to be kind and respectful in a position of competitive advantage is evidence of good character.

Your Personal Strategy Preference

As you studied this brief overview, did you recognize yourself in any of these profiles more than all the others? Your individual negotiation strategy profile is different from the four-quadrant preference profile we examined in Chapter Three. That profile is unlikely to change much of the time, except in circumstances where you find yourself under significant stress or a significant life change, such as a divorce, death of a loved one, bankruptcy or a significant career change.

Your negotiation strategy profile is more fluid, and it may very well be different a few years from now based on your environment. What is more important here is that your strategy in any negotiation will need to reflect the demands of the circumstances rather than only reflecting your preferences. Therefore, to move to the next level of negotiation competence, you must develop a keen awareness of your defaults so that you can bring intentional design to your negotiations. For example, you may not be comfortable right now approaching a negotiation in a competitive mode, but there will likely be circumstances where it is the most appropriate choice, and you will need to be able to operate in it.

Negotiation Strategies In Action

You're likely familiar with the Pareto Principle a.k.a., the "productivity principle," or the "80/20 Rule," where twenty percent of your activity contributes eighty percent of the value. It applies to the consideration of negotiation as well.

The Highest-Value Relationships

For the twenty percent of your interactions that yield the bulk of your organization's value, I suggest you take a collaborative approach. Look for ways to maximize these high-value deals and relationships in new and creative ways. Build partnerships and coalitions around mutually beneficial outcomes. These high-value, strategic transactions are where you want to be genuinely innovative.

Time-Wasting Interactions

The next twenty percent of your interactions are probably just wasting your time. There's little or no profit in these engagements, no future in them, and they frankly don't make sense in your overall objectives. As a matter of fact, this kind of business would be great business to give to your competitors; let them tie up their resources with them. Why continue to invest your time, money, and resources in these negotiations? Let it go and avoid these interactions.

Interactions With Real Potential

Maybe another twenty percent of what you're busy with holds potential, but you don't have established credentials in that area. Perhaps it's an area of development you are pursuing, but you haven't assembled a track record you can use to promote yourself yet. In those cases, you're going to have to look for ways to be accommodating, satisfying other people's needs first to establish the relationship. You will have to create some value before you can claim value.

Good, But Not Great

There will be another twenty percent of your deals that is already profitable and holds some promise but probably will never turn into the most significant thing you do. It is a sweet spot where you get a good return on your efforts so you can be compromising in your approach.

A Position Of Relative Power

Finally, there will be the last twenty percent of your negotiations where the margin is acceptable or even desirable, and you hold a strong market position (such as when you are the only provider of an end of life product or spare part). It's probably never going to grow into something else, but you have a strong position that allows you to be competitive in your approach (another reminder that a competitive approach must always be an approach that still dignifies, respects and honors your counterpart).

The Power Of Mastering All Five Strategies

To join the ranks of elite level negotiators, you must predetermine the negotiation approach you will follow in any situation because you have limited resources available. It's not smart to try to shoehorn a collaborative approach into negotiations you need to avoid, as you will be robbing your strategic opportunities of valuable resources. Equally, if you're competitive where you need to be accommodating, that's not smart either, as it could burn bridges.

The more adept you are with utilizing each of the negotiation strategies, the more pleasant, productive, and profitable your relationships will be.

This is why it is critical that you bring design to the way you negotiate; you need to move away from relying only on your defaults. There is no linear approach to negotiating. Returning to the golf analogy, how do you decide which club you're going to use? You look at the situation. You don't see the pros walking down the fairway already picking the club they're going to hit. They walk up to the ball, evaluate the situation, then choose a club to get the best result for that position in those conditions.

You are going to do the same thing with your negotiations from now on: assess the situation, conditions, the long-term value of the relationships, and relative strengths and weaknesses, and only then decide which strategy to pursue.

Choosing The Right Strategy

What your preferred negotiation style points out to you is your default mode of engagement; this is the golf club you reach for without even looking at the situation. It's going to work sometimes, but it's never going to be the right club all the time. You want to get good at discerning when you should be using each strategy.

Now that we've examined the five fundamental negotiation strategies in detail, let's look at three key questions you should ask yourself during the planning process to determine the most appropriate strategy for your negotiation:

How Many Alternatives Do You Have At Your Disposal?

When you have many equally attractive alternative options available, then you don't have to stick with one option; you can go to somebody else. So when you have many ways of solving a problem, it allows you to be more assertive.

Going back to the office supply example, if you have ten possible vendors to choose from, you have more leverage to ask for a lower price or better terms than if there were only one vendor in town. Walmart has built an empire largely based on this one factor: they can demand the best price and terms from their vendors because everyone wants them to carry their products.

By contrast, the fewer or less attractive your alternatives, the more cooperative you will have to be. If there are only two vendors who carry the parts you need, and one is in another country or charges twice as much for the same components, you will have less room to demand special consideration from the other.

This is why professional buyers will sometimes scan the entire global market to ensure that they have as many alternatives available as possible and do not become reliant on one supplier only. On the other hand, if you have no options and your counterpart is the only game in town, you're going to end up being more accommodating.

How Important Is The Relationship To You?

I find this question fascinating. Over the past seventeen years, I've worked with literally hundreds of companies all over the world and in all this time I've never worked with a company that hasn't told me that relationships are key to their success. I have yet to discover a company that says, "Actually, we're just here to make money. We don't care about people or relationships." But is that true in practice?

The next time you engage with a new business for the first time, ask them what they would say are their top differentiators. I'll bet you all the money I have in my wallet one of the top three differentiators they will mention is their people.

The thing is, most people don't mean what they are saying when they say people are their top differentiator. To offer some perspective, let's look at relationship counseling. You may have been through some rough patches in your relationships, maybe even a divorce. I have. Do you know what happens? When there's no cooperativeness, if you don't meet people's needs, then relationships will end. Relationships don't advance when people feel that their needs are not being met. So, if relationships are important to you, then you will have no choice but to be cooperative.

So, imagine my surprise when companies tell me they value people and relationships and then default to a highly assertive, uncooperative, and competitive negotiation style.

Often, the professional buyers I work with believe they're going to get concessions and better deals from sellers if they are assertive or aggressive, so they beat the vendors over the head with the figurative "price hammer." The main problem with this approach is that it doesn't recognize and harness what we know about human nature to get the best long-term deals. If this is your approach, the Rule of Reciprocity says they will catch on to your game eventually and make sure they respond in kind, through hidden margins, price inflation, or other hidden tactics to protect their interests, as it is clear to them that you have no regard for their interests.

If it is important to you to establish or maintain a good relationship with your counterpart after you have reached an agreement, then you will want to satisfy as many of their interests, goals, and objectives as you can. If your counterpart could be a good source of referrals for you, then it would be wise to cultivate that relationship, even if it means giving up some things that might otherwise be important to you, like your price. Some might call that a "losing" position, but is it?

On the other hand, I think of my experiences dealing with TV/cable/internet service providers in different cities where I've lived: some have given the undeniable impression that they didn't care if I continued doing business with them. You may have had a similar experience. It is their prerogative to be assertive and uncooperative in setting the terms with me because they have many customers and few or no competitors.

You may think that you only negotiate during the interaction to close the deal, but that's not the case. You still must implement and manage (and sometimes mend) the deal. In reality, you are negotiating from the first encounter with your counterpart up to the last time you have to address the issues that have arisen with that counterpart's project.

A lot of vendors are brilliant; they know the buyer is going to drive hard when making the deal, so they get even during the implementation or support stages. If the buyer tries to put in a service-level request or change anything on the agreement, they are going to reclaim their dignity at the buyer's expense, and the buyer is going to feel the Rule of Reciprocity in full effect.

How do you feel when you're negotiating and your counterpart treats you with a lack of respect and dignity? You don't feel like helping them achieve their goals, do you? Most people are far more likely, whether a buyer or seller, to give you a better deal if you treat them with dignity and respect in a spirit of cooperation.

One of the six principles of persuasive communication identified by Dr Robert Cialdini in his groundbreaking research is what he calls the ***Liking Principle:*** we prefer to do business with people we like. So, who are you going to offer a better deal to? Somebody you like or somebody you dislike? It's a no-brainer. It seems like total common sense. Yet that bit of common sense seems to be very uncommon in the formal business sector.

Perhaps the fact that we've built these big organizations to hide in allows us, on a subconscious level, to do worse evils than we would do if we were working for ourselves. The trend since the late 1980s has been a gradual (but accelerating) erosion of trust within the global business environment. It's an institutional thing that I have observed due to, among other things, these vast, multinational enterprises with millions of employees that we've built.

How Much Time Do You Have To Render A Decision?

What would you do if you have all the time in the world to make a decision? Well, you can do just about anything, can't you? But if you don't have time to investigate and weigh all your options, you're going to end up taking a more accommodating posture to secure the best immediate choice. I can think of a couple of instances at airport ticket counters where I needed to catch the next available flight out and did not have the luxury of time to negotiate a lower fare.

Think about those three factors as you pick your strategy:

- If the relationship is crucial to you, your time is limited, or you don't have many alternatives, that is not the time to be assertive. Your better choice would be to find areas of compromise and look for opportunities to collaborate.

- If many different options are available to you, there's no time pressure to act, and the relationship isn't strategically critical, it gives you more room to be more assertive and less cooperative.

The Power of Strategy

When we take the time to develop a strategy in advance of a negotiation, we get to design the way we're going to interact. When the inevitable curveball comes, you will not be swayed because your overall strategy is in place and that structure gives you the flexibility to respond adroitly, regardless of what your counterpart does or doesn't do. You are now the master of your destiny. No matter how important a contract may be to you, give yourself the freedom to follow your plan, even if it means to walk away empty-handed. Let your strategy and plan direct your actions. Then you are truly in control of your own destiny.

If you let other people's behaviors determine yours, your results will never be better than average. The saying is true, "you can only change yourself; you can't change other people." By bringing design to your negotiations, you harness the Rule of Reciprocity to work powerfully for you instead of working against you, because you are setting an example for others to follow or reciprocate.

How To Strengthen Your Default Strategy

Now that you have identified your default negotiation strategy, let's review the strengths and weaknesses of each so you can maximize the power of your default mode before we begin sharpening your skill with the others.

Once again, none of these strategy preferences is better than the others. That's why I prefer to distance it from the "win/lose" model; there are too many negative connotations that add baggage to the discussions.

It's kind of like if you're in the military. Which branch is the best: Army? Navy? Air Force? It depends where the battle is, right? If the fight is at sea, the army might not be as useful as the navy. Ultimately, the best strategy is the one that will get the best results right now. As we've already observed, avoiding isn't always the worst, and collaborating isn't always the best.

Competitive

If your default negotiation strategy is competitive, you will benefit from asking more questions, and not just any questions. Once again, it can't be linear. You should choose open-ended questions to expose your counterparts' interests. Often, if you have a strong preference for a competitive strategy, the questions you will tend to ask will be leading questions that focus on validating your own needs, rather than questions that allow you to understand what matters to your counterpart. Closed or leading questions typically guide your counterparts to give you the information you want to hear rather than using open questions to expose what really motivates them.

The good news is, if you're highly competitive, it is unlikely that other people won't know what you want; it's tough for you not to tell them what you need, so you're naturally going to find a way for them to understand what's important to you. All I'm suggesting you do is change the sequence, by exposing their interests at the front of the conversation.

Make a conscious effort from the heart to be sincere in your questioning. Don't be one who asks a question without listening for the answer, simply waiting for your turn to speak.

Can You Be Both Competitive and Assertive?

Periodically, a participant in one of my negotiation workshops will raise their hand and say that they scored high in both compete and accommodate. That seems counterintuitive because those profiles are opposites to each other. This simply means that, when you feel something is essential, you get protective and determined about it, but when it's not as important, you give it up. It's a matter of relative value. If this is you, the mindset you need to bring to the table is, this may not be of much value to me, but it might be of significant value to my counterpart. If it's potentially important to them, I shouldn't just let it go. I might be able to use that to my advantage later.

Accommodating

Now, let's consider the accommodators. While they might seem like the people you always want across the table from you, they can cause similar problems from a different angle. While competitive negotiators often leave people feeling like they've been taken advantage of, people who default to accommodating have the opposite problem. They are so interested in satisfying other people's needs at their own expense that it builds up resentment over time. They feel taken advantage of and neglected, even though they created the situation for themselves by giving up too much, and eventually, they explode. And everyone else is left scratching their heads, perplexed.

Often, accommodators lack the skill or the confidence to express what their own needs are. Sometimes they feel unworthy to receive benefits, or they have a "martyr complex." Neither is useful. People can't satisfy your needs if they don't know what they are. To strengthen your position, you must be willing to let people know what is essential to you. Find a line you will not allow others to cross and stick to it. Then move it forward gradually. Communicating your needs is an essential life skill.

Avoiding

Years ago, when I started out in business I could be categorized as an avoider. Over the years, experience has taught me that if you have a high preference for avoiding, it is typically for one of two reasons:

1. You avoid negotiations because you would like to avoid conflict.

2. You avoid negotiations because it is simply unimportant to you.

When I was in the corporate world, I was not a very good manager. I have had quite a few people working for me over the years, and I had a reputation that I would hire people and then turn and fire them just as quickly. I didn't do the management bit in the middle because I believed I hired people because they were qualified to do the job and I shouldn't have to teach them the job. That's poor leadership development.

But the truth is that I was avoiding the daily negotiation of management. I didn't want to have those difficult conversations. I didn't want to have to give direction or correction. Their performance (or my evaluation of it) would deteriorate over time and I would get fed up and fire them, without ever having let them know anything was wrong. I never took the time to show them the difference between what they were doing and what I expected. Naturally, they were almost always blindsided, and they were quite right. The very least you can expect from your manager is to receive regular, honest feedback. I never did that well because I was avoiding it. My avoidance preference was costing everyone time and money.

So, there were two aspects of my avoidance that had to change:

- Small problems left unaddressed would metastasize to the point that they were out of control, and I would fire people, seemingly at random. I had to learn to actively confront things that were out of sync with my expectations.

- I carried an aura of being aloof and dismissive because I wouldn't act on things that other people felt were important, if they weren't important to me.

That was also a challenge for me; it was a point of significant personal development, which is critical for being a successful leader. I had to work on those things so that when people raise issues to me, even though I'd rather avoid it, I will take the time to explore the situation and actively pursue good outcomes, at least to validate their concerns. Passivity is destructive in business, particularly in leadership, and avoidance does not build or sustain healthy relationships.

Having said all that, there are times when actively avoiding negotiation is useful, especially if you are a chronic collaborator. If you prefer collaborating, you likely are overcommitted because you feel like you need to be actively involved in everything that comes across your desk. You can probably identify situations where it is not productive (or may even be counterproductive) for you to be involved, and choose instead to avoid.

Collaborative

I have observed many people who have a strong preference for a collaborative approach overinvest in negotiations. In business, you have limited resources. If you want to become everyone's hero and solve everyone's needs, unfortunately, you deny your shareholders the value they should expect. You should be developing deep collaborative relationships with a handful of key counterparts that can move the enterprise forward toward the achievement of strategic objectives, and not every stakeholder that fits that description. Focus is the key to maximizing your collaborative strength.

Compromise

If you have a high preference for compromise, you probably tend to grab the deal too soon. You may take the first offer where you feel like you've got some of what you want, and you don't stay in the game long enough to realize the full potential of the deal. It can be useful at times to seek a baseline exchange, but there is usually more to be had than what your counterpart is showing, so my recommendation would be to hang in there a bit longer. It has been said that, until your counterpart starts saying no, there is still unexploited value on the table.

Changing Modes

As you learn the strengths of each strategy and begin practicing them in real-world scenarios, you will likely find that your default will change. Your environment can also influence it. The typical profile of sellers, according to the profiles we observed using the Thomas-Kilmann Conflict Mode Instrument (TKI), is compromising, while the average profile of buyers is competitive.

It's common for people who switch from the buy side to the sell side to also shift their default mode. In a way, that can be counterproductive. When I work on the buy side, I equip people to be more collaborative, but when I work on the sell side, I endeavor to get people to be more assertive and competitive. Why would I do that? Because when you are fluent in your counterpart's native mode, you can communicate with them more deftly.

If you find yourself moving from a buying position to a selling position or vice versa, take some of what has made you successful across the table with you. I think you will find that your negotiations are smoother and less confrontational, as you will see from your counterparts' perspective more easily.

Automation Is Moving the Needle Toward Avoidance

I would say that the majority of business deals falls into the compete, compromise, or accommodate categories. These are modes of negotiation where people interact directly and the most mutually satisfying deals come to fruition. To a lesser degree, the collaborative mode is a desirable aspiration to pursue, but it has its limits in the business environment.

A major trend I see developing is the steady increase in avoidance behaviors in the form of e-auctions, e-procurement, and similar automated systems. There's no haggling when you're dealing with a machine (not yet, anyway).

You may have observed that more of your daily transactions are in the "take it or leave it" space. Interactions that used to involve in-person visits are now on e-auction; you simply load your rates, and the activity flows from there. You have no way of knowing what the competition is doing or what difficulties or new needs the client has.

In many ways, it's a race to the bottom, with the least possible human interaction. We've already seen some industries removing humans from the interaction—first, the vending machine, now touch-screens at McDonald's. In the corporate world, we see fewer face-to-face meetings and more email, phone calls, video calls, and webinars. In using these modes of communication, you lose so much of the insight and understanding that comes from non-verbal communication. Even video conferencing is not much better than the telephone. I'll address that in more detail later in the book.

People tend to think that they save money by doing these things, but in reality, you're extending the negotiation cycle, particularly when it involves cross-cultural negotiations. It's easy to weigh the cost of a plane ticket to China against the value of the sale, but when you remove the non-verbal communication, you amplify the opportunities for misunderstanding. Call me old-fashioned, but no matter the technological advance, you will almost always get the deal done more quickly and more advantageously to both parties when you engage face-to-face than over a wire.

I'm not alone in my assessment. High performers almost always work face-to-face. You won't see the CEO of any reputable Fortune 100 company negotiating primarily via email. They will invite their counterparts to meet in person. Certainly, there are CEOs out there who don't like to get their hands dirty because it's not their blood, sweat, and tears invested in the birth and growth of the company, so they send colleagues to work out the finer points of deals.

That's not the norm among founders. Richard Branson is not going to delegate mission critical negotiations to his lieutenants; he engages personally. Warren Buffet understands the importance of face-to-face engagements. He does not leave critical partnerships to the cold austerity of an online transaction. And he has the results to show for it.

Does What Your Counterpart Sees Match Your Intent?

I haven't yet heard a businessperson say, "Our model is to be competitive. We are dismissive of anyone outside ourselves." Rather, everybody says, "We're about partnership." or "We're all about collaboration." But then they stick in the knife and demand price concessions.

Perception is what governs our understanding; not intent. The quality of your communication skill is measured by how your counterpart understands what you said, not by what you meant. Often, companies who say they intend to be collaborative bring a competitive approach to everything.

This is why you need first to select what strategy you wish to pursue and then make sure that your tactics, approach, and model of engagement are consistent with that intention. In a word, it's all about managing your counterpart's perception.

What does your behavior look like when you are truly collaborative? Or how do you know that the party across the table from you intends to be collaborative? Some clues might be:

- They engage you with solid eye contact
- Their body posture is open and welcoming
- They don't talk only about themselves, but rather about you (this might be the clearest clue)
- They ask you open questions about your interests and goals
- They will often make themselves vulnerable by also sharing their vital interests—even their weaknesses—freely

What about people in the competitive mode? What does it look like when they sit across the table from you?

- They sit down and start listing their needs and requirements without asking yours
- They offer you free consultancy by telling you what you should be doing in setting up your business so it can serve them better

Many organizations have a reputation for doing this. They then expect the people across the table to be collaborative or accommodating in response, which then does not transpire.

Use The Rule of Reciprocity to Foster Collaboration

If you desire to be collaborative, you need to activate the Rule of Reciprocity in that direction. Remember that reciprocity is an overarching principle underpinning human behavior, where we return to others the form of behavior that they exhibit toward us.

If you want to signal that you're collaborative, you should start the conversation by talking about your counterpart's needs and interests and let reciprocity drive them to respond by talking about you.

I've often seen people have collaborative intent, but then start by talking about themselves and their needs, so their counterpart is then incentivized to reciprocate and talk about themselves. But if I've invested time cooperating with you by listening to you, eventually, you're going to listen to me, too.

The Power Of The Vulnerability Risk

Another curious human characteristic is the way we so often use the wrong evidence from our past to motivate our behavior for the future. I think it is fair to say that all of us have been taken advantage of at some point in our lives, because we made ourselves vulnerable to someone. Because of that negative experience, we say we don't ever want to make ourselves vulnerable again. That's not unreasonable. Yet research suggests that the number of people who would never take advantage of you is far greater than the handful of people who have done so.

In my own experience, far more people have moved in my direction because I made myself vulnerable than have taken advantage of me. We offer a full money-back guarantee on all products and services that we deliver, which many companies won't do for fear of being exploited. The fact is, only once in 18 years did anyone claim their money back, and the employee responsible for that was exposed as short cutting and released. We are protected because reciprocity demands they recognize the value of what we've done for them.

When you think about it, someone who is going to take advantage of you is probably going to take advantage of you regardless of whether you make yourself vulnerable or not. So some claiming their money back most likely decided that they wanted to take advantage of the money back offer to get free access to our training and resources even before they signed up.

The same is true in negotiation: the overwhelming majority of people will never take advantage of you when you put their interests first. It takes courage to take that step, but it's always well worth it.

If your counterpart throws down the gauntlet in a competitive way and you respond competitively, you will perpetuate the competitive tone. It will never move toward compromise or collaboration. You will only maintain the status quo.

Your responsibility here—and this requires courage—is to respond in a way that *violates* reciprocity. You have to decide, "I'm not going to fall victim to the Rule of Reciprocity. I'm going to recast this exchange and then harness reciprocity in support of what I want to achieve here."

This is why it is so important that you decide before you go in what mode of negotiation you're going to be using, and why.

Don't Let Your Counterpart Steer

Imagine you have a counterpart who tends to come across in an adversarial, competitive way, and there has been a legacy of competitive engagement between the two of you. Now, having read this, you decide to give it a fling and try doing things differently—to put the other person first. The first time you approach them in a more compromising way, they will likely think, "What's going on here? Are they trying to sucker me?"

Why? Because this new behavior is inconsistent with what you've done before. So they are going to respond accordingly. After it doesn't work once or twice, you will likely give up and revert to your old style. Then your counterpart will feel validated in their opinion that you were trying to sucker them. This is not the way that you want to go about it.

Sales research suggests that you will have a hard time saying "no" more than seven times to an offer. The mistake so many people make is they give up too soon. To harness the Rule of Reciprocity in your favor will require you to be consistent in deploying your new behavior. Consistency is almost always the difference between the successful person and the unsuccessful one. The fortune is in the follow-up, as the old saying goes.

If I am consistent in embracing the new negotiation strategy mode, regardless of what my counterpart does, over time they're going to realize that this new behavior model is authentic, and they will adjust accordingly.

The Genius of Mandela

This is exactly what President Nelson Mandela did when he led negotiations to establish democratic rule in South Africa. He set the tone for the kind of compromising and collaborative negotiation process that he wished to pursue with the former apartheid government. In one of his first interviews after being released from twenty-seven years being held as a political prisoner, he publicly declared his and his political party's willingness to compromise.

Now think about that. Consider some of the other chronic political standoffs, in places like Ireland, the Middle East, and the Koreas. Typically, one side says, "You will free our people from jail and give up your weapons first before we even engage with you." What's the predictable response they get? "No, you'll have to make a concession first."

Instead, President Mandela said, "We're happy to compromise; we're happy to give up on some of our demands." The South African government could hardly come back and say, "Yes, you'll be the only ones compromising."

Instead, the government said, "We, too, will compromise." Mandela was a negotiation genius. What he did was completely counterintuitive, and it worked. His biggest challenge was his constituents. His own people said to him, "Are you mad? How can you make that kind of gesture? It's payback time."

If you want to perform at an elite level of negotiation competence, you're going to have to do some counterintuitive things that eighty percent of people will tell you is stark raving mad. It's counterintuitive to be exceedingly successful, so you will have to decide between wishing to be an average negotiator only doing that which others do or being an elite level negotiator. You may wish to be healthy, to have successful relationships, or to be a great negotiator; but wishing is not enough. It is only action that moves you to take the uncomfortable steps required to leave the status quo and move into destiny. If it were comfortable, everyone would do it. You cannot grow and be comfortable at the same time.

President Mandela spent his time in prison preparing for this one negotiation: he learned to speak Afrikaans, the language of his counterpart. He didn't just learn to speak it a little; he developed his skill until he could understand Afrikaans poetry. He studied to understand the psyche of his counterparts. If you haven't seen the movie **Invictus**, I highly recommend that you watch it. It's a very good reflection of the man.

I worked briefly with Dr David Venter, Former Director General of Communications for the South African Government under President Mandela. Before that, he had held the same office for the apartheid government under President F.W. de Klerk. When President Mandela took over, he asked David to stay on, which was, of course, the surprise of the century for David.

To close this chapter, I want to share with you one of the numerous stories Dr Venter shared with me about President Mandela.

Just after he got elected president, there was a press conference at his home in Cape Town. The press wanted to catch a glimpse of him after his first few days in power. This home has a large driveway and plaza with a large fountain in the middle. Hundreds of reporters waited in the plaza. One journalist stood on the edge of the fountain to get a better view, and as Mandela came to the door, there was a huge push forward, and he fell into the shallow fountain.

What happened next will truly give you an insight into the character of President Mandela. He saw the man fall in, walked through the crowd of reporters, extended his hand, and he pulled him out of the fountain. Then he turned to his handlers and instructed, "Why don't you take him inside, give him something dry to wear? I will give him a private opportunity to take as many pictures as he wants." What other world leader have you ever seen do something like that? Most are too "important" to stoop to meet a common man in his moment of need. That's how President Mandela engendered the almost universal reverence he receives from around the world.

As you seek to violate the Rule of Reciprocity and engage your counterparts in a way that honors them, you will find the respect and admiration of others directed to you and greater success in all your negotiations.

Key Takeaways from Chapter Four

- There are five primary strategies of negotiation that fall across a spectrum on two axes: assertiveness and cooperation.

- Every person has a default negotiation strategy that they apply instinctively in every interaction.

- A key to success as a negotiator is to increase your facility in applying all five strategies where they are appropriate.

- Our world is gradually moving away from human interaction toward "take it or leave it" automated transactions. In doing so, we are squelching the non-verbal signals that foster greater collaboration and opportunity to serve each other's unspoken interests.

- Successful negotiators use the Rule of Reciprocity to lead their counterpart to move in their direction. This requires some vulnerability, but the reward is greater than the risk.

> *"The best move you can make in negotiation is to think of an incentive the other person hasn't even thought of, and then meet it."*

—Eli Broad

Apply It To Your Situation

1. Identify three things you learned from this chapter that you want to begin implementing in your negotiations. Highlight the one you want to do first.

   _____

   _____

   _____

   _____

2. Describe how you see the five strategic negotiation modes operating in your life.

   _____

   _____

   _____

   _____

3. Describe a relationship where you have been operating in one strategy, and you would benefit from changing to a different strategy. What would you do differently in that new strategy?

   _____

   _____

   _____

   _____

4. What did you learn about strategy and planning that surprised or enlightened you?

   _____

   _____

   _____

   _____

Chapter Five: Tactics

Executive Summary

- Within any negotiation strategy is a palette of tactics that aligns with the strategic goal.

- Tactics fall into two main categories: integrative and distributive, each of which fosters a different atmosphere for negotiation.

- Some tactics may be considered pushy or even unethical. Our point in this book is not to advocate for their use, but to help you recognize when they are being used against you.

- It is important to differentiate between your counterparts' choice of tactics and their character or emotional state.

From Strategy To Tactics

Once you've chosen your strategy for the negotiation, you should plan your specific action steps or tactics.

I often encounter confusion about what negotiation strategy and tactics are and how they should work together. Many people don't know what either of these terms means; some people think they are strictly military terms. Others simplify them to a construct where strategy means "long-term" and tactics means "short-term," which isn't a helpful way to think of them. Your strategy could change in the course of a single meeting, but you might have a preferred tactic that you employ consistently.

I like to think of it this way:

Imagine you were visiting the United States for the first time and had never seen a National Football League game before. You switch on the television and see twenty-two grown men in brightly colored battle gear beating the daylights out of each other in the middle of a striped grass field.

Without someone to give you context, you would have no idea what was going on. But, as you watch and listen to the plays, you will begin to identify who the teams are and what each team's goals are. As you grow your competence and understanding of the rules of the game, you learn the difference between the offense and defense and their strategies. Over time, you begin to recognize the different positions, field placements, and plays they run. Now you are seeing the game at a tactical level.

If you were to play the game for a while, you would learn how to form a plan that includes an overall strategy for the game and a tactical playbook. As your skill increases and you move into a coaching role, you learn to analyze the opposing team's strengths, weaknesses, and preferred tactics, and build measures into your game plan so that you can stick to your strategy and not spend the whole game in a reactive posture, being led around by what the other team does.

The great Chinese commander Sun Tzu explained it this way: "All the men can see the tactics I use to conquer, but what none can see is the strategy out of which great victory is evolved."

Strategy Is The Context For Tactics

Your strategy for the negotiation must be identified first, to give context to the tactics you will employ. A mistake I frequently see negotiators make is that they use a tactic that doesn't fit their strategy, because they saw someone do it effectively in another. Just as your objectives must inform your strategy, your tactics must flow naturally out of your strategy.

If you intend to be competitive (and don't care if you ever see your counterpart again), then I have some good news for you: you can use all of these tactics as you see fit. However, as you move to some of the other strategies to become more cooperative and less assertive, your selection of tactics becomes more restricted.

Two Categories of Tactics

Tactics fall into two main categories:

- Integrative tactics, which are typically used to create and foster accommodating, compromising, or collaborative negotiation environments.

- Distributive tactics, which are used to create and foster competitive negotiation environments or when we want to avoid negotiations altogether.

Dealing with Tactics

While you are planning your tactics, you can be sure that your professional negotiation counterpart is preparing their own. If you're negotiating in the corporate world, you will inevitably have tactics used against you, including some that you may consider unethical or manipulative. Just as you must have a toolkit of tactics at the ready, it is essential to be able to identify the tactics your counterpart is using and have the knowledge and skills to counteract them effectively.

The approaches detailed below have one other crucial thing in common: they all separate the *tactics* from the *person*. When your counterpart employs a tactic—especially one that you find offensive or manipulative—it can affect your perception of them and have a detrimental impact on the negotiation. It is advisable not to focus on this behavior, but rather consider the possible reasons for the approach.

Never define an individual by the tactics he or she employs. Branding somebody a "manipulator" because they chose a tactic that felt negatively manipulative will not help the negotiation process. Negotiators sometimes act out of habit, without giving proper thought to their actions. Have you ever done that and regretted it?

At other times, what we perceive as a tactic may be a symptom of an underlying interest. A friend who is a professional counselor has described to me how angry or hurting people may lash out in a way that has nothing to do with the conversation or the person they attacked but reveals a pain point that hadn't been identified before. Similarly, your counterpart may respond to something you've said in a way that seems inappropriate on the surface, but if you pause and assess where that response came from, you might be able to identify an underlying interest they hadn't disclosed before. By choosing not to let the tactic offend you, you have the opportunity and the composure available to surface that unmet need and address it.

Think about that: you might change the outcome of the negotiation, the relationship with your counterpart, and your career, only by having the presence of mind to distinguish the tactic from the person.

Common Negotiation Tactics And How To Use Them

There are many tactics and ploys used in negotiation. In this section, we will cover the tactics most often used within a commercial context. You will note that each description contains an indication of the strategies it supports.

CAVEAT: I want to make sure I am clear here: some of these tactics are going to seem unethical or negatively manipulative to you, and you are right to feel that way about them. My point in sharing them with you is not to advocate for their use but to equip you to recognize when they are deployed against you, so you can formulate an appropriate response or countermeasure—and this is key—without becoming a victim of reciprocity. There is an old expression among negotiators that states, "You should never approach the negotiation table pointing a gun, but you should always know where the guns are."

I am often amused when I watch the evening news and see some of these tactics employed by politicians or activists. As you study them, you will likely recall times when you have seen them used. That will anchor the image in your mind so that you will recognize it in real negotiation scenarios. Some of the names we have assigned to these tactics might be different from what you might have heard them called in the past. Don't let that distract you. The point is to recognize the behavior and internalize an appropriate response.

The Puppy Dog

Compatible With These Strategies

Collaborate, Compromise, Accommodate, Compete.

What It Looks Like

Allowing your counterpart to experience the product, solution, or service that you are proposing before closing a deal. Many local animal shelters give a two-week "family fit" trial where the customer gets to keep the puppy long enough to form a bond. Like bringing a new puppy into your home, the longer your customer has to get comfortable with the new arrangement, the more attached they will become.

Example

Software provided as a free trial for thirty days with no obligation to buy.

How To Deal With The Puppy Dog

Make sure that you agree with all the possible terms and agreements before participating in trying out the free product, service, or solution. Once you decide to buy the product, service or solution based on your experience with it, you are likely to pay more than you would have if you didn't try it first due to your perception of the reduction in the quality of the available alternatives.

The Trade-Off

Compatible With These Strategies

Collaborate, Compromise, Accommodate, Compete.

What It Looks Like

Any time your counterpart tries to renegotiate terms, or there is a change to an agreement due to the other party's fault, there is an opportunity to ask the other side to compensate for the difference.

Example

"I understand that things have changed on your side and that you didn't plan things to end up this way. I will try my best to convince my boss, but I will need something to give her as she had given her sign-off based on what we discussed earlier. What can you give me to compensate?"

How To Deal With The Trade-Off

Always make sure that you enter negotiations with high aspirations so that you can make concessions if you need to. The principle of reciprocity will play an important role here. If you are asked to concede due to things changing on your side, you should clearly state the fact that you are prepared to concede since things changed. This should serve as a precedent moving forward.

The Set Aside

Compatible With These Strategies

Collaborate, Compromise, Compete, Avoid

What It Looks Like

When faced with a complicated issue, you might try to ignore the problem, park it for the time being, and move on to another point.

Example

"Why don't we come back to this later on and first explore the key reasons you want to pursue this project?"

How To Deal With The Set Aside

Politely point out to your counterpart that the issue is of critical importance to you and that it is not possible to talk about other points until you're able to understand the point they're trying to set aside fully. "I agree that we should also explore the key reasons why we want to pursue this project, but before we can do that we need to understand this key point. Otherwise, it might be difficult for us to get the resources we need to ensure the success of any potential project."

Association

Compatible With These Strategies

Collaborate, Compromise, Accommodate, Compete

What It Looks Like

People like to do business with well-connected people. Position yourself as an expert in your counterpart's industry by presenting testimonials, references, and associations with esteemed companies and individuals.

Example

"The last time I spoke with Bill Gates, he asked me the same question. He faced similar issues to what you're facing, and he contracted us to take care of it. This is how we addressed his issues."

How To Deal With Association

You have to be aware that you will be more likely to move in your counterpart's direction if they can offer examples of people or organizations that you respect as having taken similar action to what they would like you to consider. Be cautious about name-dropping, however, unless you know for sure that your association will stand up to scrutiny.

Funny Money

Compatible With These Strategies

Compromise, Compete

What It Looks Like

Offering financial arrangements that make it appear that the price is lower than it is. This is often done by spreading the cost over time (buy now, pay later).

Example

"You've made a great decision. Let's complete the lease agreement, but before we get started, I should mention that for only $10 per week, you can add the service plan. The amount is so small you probably won't even notice it."

How To Deal With Funny Money

Make sure that you state upfront that agreement is dependent on agreeing on all terms. In other words, there is no agreement until there is agreement on all terms. You could also use Funny Money in reverse—for example: 'Does the lease agreement include the service plan?'

Print & Policies

Compatible With These Strategies

Collaborate, Compromise, Compete

What It Looks Like

People lend more weight to the written word and company policies than just the spoken word.

Example

"I'm sorry, this is just company policy. I'm not able to move outside of the parameters allowed by the policy."

How To Deal With Print & Policies

You could ask very diplomatically if you could be sent a copy of the policy to help your internal discussions. In some cases, when you do this, you will notice that a way can be found around the policy issue. If your counterpart does send you a copy of their policy, you can respond by asking what the process is to review and change the policy or what has been done in the past to gain exceptions to policies.

The Vice

Compatible With These Strategies

Compete

What It Looks Like

Continuously asking for unreciprocated concessions until your counterpart refuses to make any more concessions.

Example

"Thank you for your proposal. I've spoken to our finance director, and we would like you to improve your offer." After the other side comes back with a price reduction, the process is repeated. "Thank you for the improvement in price. Unfortunately, we need you to sharpen your price some more."

How To Deal With The Vice

Whenever you are asked to improve your offer, you have to respond by asking for a target or a budget. For example: "Thank you for your feedback. I'm not sure that we're able to improve our offer, as it already is our best offer. What is your budget so that I can take this back to my colleagues to workshop whether something could be done to bridge the gap?"

Planted Information

Compatible With These Strategies

Compete

What It Looks Like

You are probably often presented with information that is not strictly true by your counterparts, and it can appear to be especially compelling if the information is learned by chance rather than explicitly provided by your counterpart themselves.

Example

One of your counterpart's team members passes a note to one of their team members stating more favorable terms than what you're offering. During a break, they leave the note lying on the table so you can see it.

How To Deal With Planted Information

Be aware that planted information will serve to anchor your expectations. Being adequately prepared is your best defense against planted information. Specifically, you should be very familiar with the competitive landscape so that you significantly reduce the likeliness of falling prey to this tactic.

The Hot Potato

Compatible With These Strategies

Collaborate, Compromise, Compete

What It Looks Like

Your counterpart attempts to make their problem your problem in the hope that you will assume responsibility for solving it.

Example

"We would love to move ahead with your $50,000 offer, but unfortunately our budget is limited to only $35,000."

How To Deal With The Hot Potato

Pass it right back. For example: "Oh, ok. If you only have $35,000, do you want to reduce the scope of work for now and take some time to see if you can increase your budget?"

The Flinch

Compatible With These Strategies

Collaborate, Compromise, Accommodate, Compete, Avoid

What It Looks Like

A physical reaction such as gasping for air or a visible expression in response to a statement, anchor, or offer.

Example

'Wow. I didn't realize that your price would be twice as high as your nearest competitor."

How To Deal With The Flinch

Make a conscious decision to expect the flinch from your counterpart, particularly when you're up against professional buyers as the flinch is "Buying 101." Often, the flinch will be followed by silence. Make sure that you don't fill the silence with a concession. Get comfortable with silence.

Limits

Compatible With These Strategies

Collaborate, Compromise, Compete

What It Looks Like

Your counterpart lets you know that they have set limits for money, time, capacity, personnel, etc.

Example

"I'm only authorized to sign off on amounts below $100,000, and the project must be delivered within a maximum of three months. If you're not able to bring your price down to below $100,000 and guarantee delivery within three months, we won't be able to proceed.'

How To Deal With Limits

You should ensure that you have leverage by creating scarcity around your recommended course of action. In other words, if there is nothing unique about your offering and suggestions, then there is no incentive for your counterpart to find a way to exceed their limit (artificial or not).

Competition

Compatible With These Strategies

Collaborate, Compromise, Accommodate, Compete

What It Looks Like

Your counterpart tells you that they have other options available.

Example

"Your competitor offered us a price that is thirty percent lower than the price you offered."

How To Deal With Competition

Professional buyers never go to a shortlist of one. You should fully expect any buyer to tell you that they have a better offer from your competitor(s). Remember that making concessions in negotiation is what creates satisfaction for your counterparts. This means you always need to leave yourself some room to make concessions. The target should not necessarily be to beat your competition's offer, but to establish value in support of your offer—while also making small concessions and demonstrating to your counterpart that you are prepared to move in their direction.

Deliberate Mistake

Compatible With These Strategies

Compete

What It Looks Like

This unethical tactic is intended to gain an unreciprocated concession from you.

Example

A seller may deliberately leave out or underprice one of the elements of a proposal.

How To Deal With The Deliberate Mistake

Don't accept this tactic. The whole negotiation should be reopened if the terms need to change in any way after an agreement has been reached. Using this tactic might very well damage the relationship beyond repair.

Cherry Picking

Compatible With These Strategies

Compromise, Compete

What It Looks Like

Buyers attempt to create their dream deal by asking for a detailed breakdown of your offer. In some cases, they may deliberately invite you to quote for more features and elements than what they are expecting to buy because they expect to get a reduced bundle price. Then, once you've submitted the offer, they ask you to break it down into its constituent parts, and they demand to pay the same price for only buying single elements of your offer.

Example

"Thank you for breaking down your cost estimate. We would like to only proceed with items A, B, and C, and won't be needing any of the other items quoted. Of course, we would expect the bundle discounted price to be kept in place for all items quoted."

How To Deal With Cherry Picking

Make sure that in your terms and conditions there is an obvious statement that says that the price quoted is conditional on purchasing the entire bundle. Even better, price each of the elements of the package at an individual rate and then clearly display the discount that is put against each item as it becomes part of the package. This way your counterpart can cherry pick all they want, and you will still make a margin on the individual elements.

Personal Attacks

Compatible With These Strategies

Compete

What It Looks Like

Personal attacks are often deliberate attempts to throw you off balance and get you to respond emotionally.

Example

"Your approach is completely amateur. You and your company cannot be trusted. Get your manager to send me someone capable of making a decision."

How To Deal With Personal Attacks

Never respond to personal attacks by defending yourself or returning the favor and attacking your counterpart personally. The best response is to reframe the negotiation or to call for an adjournment. Example: "If I were you, I probably would have said the same thing. I would like us to focus on your key objectives for a moment as I would like to invest the best effort possible in attempting to meet your needs."

Reliance On Authorities

Compatible With These Strategies

Collaborate, Compromise, Accommodate, Compete

What It Looks Like

The validity and gravity of your argument are enhanced when someone who is deemed to be an expert in the field supports the view and recommendations that you are proposing.

Example

"As you can see from the research study done by Awesome Research Company, our recommendation is in line with what the top three companies in this industry are doing."

How To Deal With Reliance On Authorities

In the first instance, you should be aware of the powerful impact of this tactic on how you view the information presented by your counterpart. Secondly, you should ensure that you highlight the issues/features that are unique to you and your organization and therefore make you less similar to the references that they are citing.

Take It Or Leave It

Compatible With These Strategies

Compete

What It Looks Like

A tactic that communicates the willingness of your counterpart to walk away from the table if certain conditions are not met.

Example

"I'm afraid that it will not be possible to reach an agreement based on the terms that you've suggested."

How To Deal With Take It Or Leave It

You have two options. If you don't have any viable alternatives available, you may have to be accommodating to ensure that you can close the deal. If you do have workable options available—or you wish to avoid creating precedents—then you should do a "soft walk away" when confronted with the take-it-or-leave-it tactic. For example: "I'm really sorry, but it doesn't look like we will be able to reach agreement on the terms proposed. We stand ready to continue discussions at any time, but fully understand that you will need to take time to review your position. If anything changes, I can commit to prioritizing our response to get the negotiation moving forward."

The Hustler

Compatible With These Strategies

Collaborate, Compromise, Accommodate, Compete

What It Looks Like

The value of a service rendered diminishes quickly after it has been delivered. In other words, a concession that you've made to your counterpart will soon lose its value if not reciprocated immediately. This means you may be asked to provide a service and then after you've delivered the service that resolved your counterpart's issues they can take all the time they need to pay you, or not even pay you at all, since their problem is now solved.

Example

"Will you please just focus on getting the project done; we can talk about the money later on."

How To Deal With The Hustler

Always ask for a reciprocal concession when you make a concession. Agree on the final price and terms before you start work. If you don't have an established relationship, don't pay upfront in full before the project commences. Stagger the payments to match completed milestones.

Precedents

Compatible With These Strategies

Collaborate, Compromise, Accommodate, Compete

What It Looks Like

A precedent serves as a guide or justification for subsequent situations. Lack of precedent can also be used as a reason for turning down an argument or specific point.

Example

"You've charged us $10 per widget for the last twelve months. There is no objective justification for a price increase." Or "I can see that you are new. You guys always offer us at least a 15% discount, as do your competitors."

How To Deal With Precedents

When you make concessions on key points, you should include a clause that states explicitly that it is a one-time concession and will not apply as a standard operating procedure in the future. You can use this to your advantage by citing previous conduct by your counterparts as justification for the course of action you wish them to pursue this time.

Good Cop/Bad Cop

Compatible With These Strategies

Compromise, Compete

What It Looks Like

The idea behind this tactic is to increase the other party's stress level on the one hand (bad cop) and induce cooperation on the other hand by using the emotional appeal (good cop).

Example

"I'm not even going to show your proposal to my boss. She's not going to be happy that your price is so much higher than all your competitors and I want to protect the relationship between our companies. I'm going to give you a chance to go and review your proposal and reduce your price substantially before I show it to her for her approval."

How To Deal With The Good Cop/Bad Cop

The first thing is that you should be aware that this is very often a planned tactic. The intent of this tactic, and all tactics for that matter, is to get you to soften your position and offer an unreciprocated concession. When you recognize this tactic, you should remember to connect any concession you may make to receiving a counter-concession of equal or similar value.

Extreme Offers

Compatible With These Strategies

Compromise, Compete

What It Looks Like

Asking for significantly more than you expect to settle for eventually. This tactic has a definite cultural connotation and is viewed as an acceptable tactic in some cultures (usually cultures where there is a tendency to allow your counterpart to save face). In Western cultures, the use of this tactic will often result in parties walking away from the negotiation.

Example

"We would expect to only pay $20,000 for this type of solution ($40,000 in reality)."

How To Deal With The Extreme Offer

If you suspect that the extreme offer tactic is being used, it is imperative that you re-anchor the outrageous offer with your own equally extreme counter-offer without defending your offer or attacking your counterpart's offer. This will create room for your counterpart to 'save face' and move in your direction. If you choose to defend your proposal or attack your counterpart's offer, then you will be very unlikely to reach an agreement.

The Trial Balloon

Compatible With These Strategies

Collaborate, Compromise, Accommodate, Compete

What It Looks Like

You float a possible solution to see if your counterpart might run with it or discard it. This is useful for exploring possibilities that could lead to closing a deal.

Example

"Would the price change if we increased the volume by thirty percent?"

How To Deal With The Trial Balloon

Should your counterpart use this tactic, it is usually a good sign that they are prepared to be at least compromising in their approach. If the suggestion doesn't meet your expectations, you could respond to the trial balloon by "floating" your own trial balloon.

Splitting The Difference

Compatible With These Strategies

Collaborate, Compromise, Compete

What It Looks Like

Agreeing to settle at a point that is halfway between your stated position and your counterpart's. It could be seen by both parties as a fair way to end discussions and display compromising behavior.

Example

"You asked for $10 per unit and our budget is $5 per unit. Shall we settle on $7.50 per unit?"

How To Deal With Splitting The Difference

If your counterpart suggests splitting the difference you can respond in one of two ways:

1. Accept their offer to split the difference, and thereby demonstrate that you are willing to compromise (this could only work if the suggested strike position is within your bargaining zone).

2. Suggest splitting the difference between their suggested amended position and your stated position, for example: "If you are prepared to pay $7.50, I would be able to split the difference between $7.50 and $10.00 and settle at $8.75."

The Decoy

Compatible With These Strategies

Compromise, Compete

What It Looks Like

A tactic used to take your counterpart's attention away from the real issue in the hope that you would offer concessions for the decoy issue. This effectively creates a fake bargaining position to get a concession from your counterpart on issues that are important to you.

Example

"I will need delivery to take place within thirty days (knowing that ninety days is the minimum delivery time)."

How To Deal With The Decoy

This tactic is particularly prevalent in contract negotiations. A demand may be made for you to agree to unreasonable guarantees in terms of liability in the full knowledge that you won't agree. This is done so that your counterparts can demand a concession from you in return for them altering that contract clause. The best thing to do if you are expecting the decoy to be used is to voice your own equally unreasonable decoy expectation in return, which may then assist you trading a red herring for a red herring.

Deferring To Higher Authority

Compatible With These Strategies

Compromise, Accommodate, Compete

What It Looks Like

Being unable to agree without the approval of someone with a higher level of authority.

Example

"Your proposal looks great; I just need to run it past my board of directors." When they come back, they state: "The board of directors won't accept your offer unless you reduce your price by fifteen percent to match the available budget."

How To Deal With The Higher Authority

When you first start your negotiations, ask the question, "In addition to you, who else needs to sign off on a final agreement?" This question honors your counterpart as being a vital part of the decision making process, yet at the same time allows you to uncover other stakeholders.

The Bottom Line

Compatible With These Strategies

Compromise, Compete

What It Looks Like

You ask your counterpart to disclose their bottom line with regards to a negotiated issue in an attempt to get them to decrease the size of their bargaining zone.

Example

"We appreciate the time you've taken with your proposal. We need something much simpler—what would be your best price for this?"

How To Deal With The Bottom Line

Hold your ground. You should let them know that you've quoted your best price possible for the conditions offered. If the price does not meet their expectations, it may be reviewed alongside other supporting conditions (payment terms, volumes, logistics, etc.).

Preconditions

Compatible With These Strategies

Compete

What It Looks Like

An attempt to gain concessions from your counterpart before the negotiation has even started. Negotiation will then (supposedly) only start based on compliance with the precondition.

Example

"We will only accept proposals from suppliers who agree to our one hundred and twenty-day payment terms."

How To Deal With Preconditions

You should indicate that you are not compliant with the preconditions but that you are happy to negotiate a transaction premised on mutual gain, should they wish to continue discussions after reviewing your proposal.

The Nibble

Compatible With These Strategies

Compromise, Accommodate, Compete

What It Looks Like

Just before the deal is closed, an additional item or request is made that seems insignificant against the overall value or context of what is being agreed.

Example

"Just before we sign off the deal, I have to let you know that our standard payment term is ninety days rather than the thirty days that you indicated in your proposal."

How To Deal With The Nibble

Make sure that you summarize the conditions upon which your offer was prepared so that no ambiguity can be exploited by your counterparts. For example, "Our price of $10,000 is based on payment terms of thirty days, delivery in seven days and subject to receiving your signed agreement by the end of this week."

Moral/Emotional Appeal

Compatible With These Strategies

Collaborate, Compromise, Accommodate, Compete

What It Looks Like

An appeal being framed as the "fair" or "right" way. The intent is to make the counterpart feel that by disagreeing with the proposal, they are unfair or politically incorrect. The tactic is designed to rely on your emotions rather than the facts that support the negotiation.

Example

"Your proposal will lead to fifty families having no income anymore. It will not make you look good, never mind the fact that the media will have a field day and you will not feel very proud of your decision."

How To Deal With The Moral/Emotional Appeal

Reframe the negotiation to bring the focus back to the reason that the negotiation is taking place in the first instance. For example, "I appreciate your insight on this matter. As we stated when we started our meeting, let's move towards agreement on terms that make sense to us both."

Delaying Or Stalling

Compatible With These Strategies

Compromise, Compete, Avoid

What It Looks Like

Delaying and stalling is a tactic that is designed to wear you out and get you to be more flexible. It can also be used when your counterpart needs more time to think or get their affairs in order.

Example

"I'm sorry, but we've had to postpone deciding on this matter for at least a month. Please send me your very best pricing proposal so that we have a clear view of where you are positioned when we meet to reach a decision in a month."

How To Deal With Delaying Or Stalling

Be aware that if you're representing a publicly-listed company, professional buyers will often postpone coming to a final agreement to the end of quarter or end of the financial year, as they know you will be more likely to offer discounts at these times. Leave yourself room to make a last-minute concession so that you don't have to move outside of your objectives when they stall until the end of the quarter. They will likely offer you the opportunity to get the deal done before the quarter closes, as long as you can make some concessions that favor them.

Bonus: eAuction

Denying your counterpart the opportunity to negotiate with you because you see what they're providing to you as a commodity.

Example

Invitations to participate in eAuctions on eProcurement platforms.

How To Deal With eAuctions

Prepare to make several concessions during the process. These concessions don't have to be significant, but you want to demonstrate that you are prepared to move in your counterpart's direction. Make sure that you don't become too emotionally involved in the process and as a result, go beyond your limits. It may even be advisable to have someone who is not involved with the deal administer the e-auction response process, as this will go a long way towards protecting you from becoming emotional in your responses and making more concessions than you planned.

Key Takeaways from Chapter Five

- Tactics should flow logically from the strategy you have chosen to employ.

- Some tactics are unethical or negatively manipulative and I do not advocate for their use, but I do want you to recognize them and be able to respond appropriately.

- It is important to separate the tactic from your counterpart's character, so you don't judge them personally based on a negotiation decision they made.

- Some behaviors are not intentional tactics at all, but emotional outbursts that could signal hidden unmet interests. Proactively and professionally manage the relationship elements of the negotiation to ensure a warm, trustworthy climate supporting all your negotiations.

> *"Litigation is about winning the argument. Negotiation is about winning the relationship."*
>
> —Jan Potgieter

Apply It To Your Situation

1. Identify three things you learned from this chapter that you want to begin implementing in your negotiations. Highlight the one you want to do first.

   _____

   _____

   _____

   _____

2. Describe how you have witnessed these tactics being used, either in the news, in a movie, or operating in your own life.

   _____

   _____

   _____

   _____

3. Describe an area of your life where you would like to see more intentional use of appropriate tactics.

   _____

   _____

   _____

   _____

4. What did you learn about negotiation in this chapter that surprised or enlightened you?

   _____

   _____

   _____

   _____

Chapter Six: Deal Objectives

Executive Summary

- The second pillar of negotiation is Value. In this pillar we quantify the goals and objectives for both parties in a specific negotiation.

- It is crucial to be clear on your objectives before entering any negotiation, including your Aspiration Base and your Real Base.

- Price and value are not the same.

- Preparation includes researching your counterparts' needs, objectives, and priorities as thoroughly as you know your own.

- Your ability to listen effectively will have dramatic impact on your success as a negotiator.

- Sometimes, the best option is to walk away from a negotiation.

- The more desirable alternatives you have going into a negotiation, the more power and confidence you will enjoy.

Pillar 2: Value

At this point, we are going to move on from the first pillar of negotiation (Vision) to the second pillar (Value). It may seem like a semantic difference, but from a strategic point of view, it is crucial to recognize the corner we've turned. We're moving past the stage where we have developed how we want the future to look, and into a stage where we concretely and measurably quantify our goals and objectives for a specific negotiation, as well as our counterparts'.

Understanding Deal Objectives

Any time I travel, whether by car across town or by airplane to another continent, the first thing I do is identify my destination. That's not rocket science. Before I pick up my keys, I have a clear and concrete view of where I am going and what I intend to accomplish. Even if I don't know the exact directions (and there may be dozens of routes available to me), I am clear on my goals for the trip, and I take along some form of guidance—my GPS, a map, or an itinerary. Unless I am keen on taking a leisurely drive through the countryside (which I should probably do more often), I have a clearly-stated objective before I leave the house.

Similarly, you should remember that negotiation is not an event, it is a process, and you are wise to enter that process with one or more clearly-stated objectives. If I were to show up at a meeting with a client or a supplier having no idea of what I hoped to achieve from that meeting, my counterpart would view me with contempt, and rightly so. It would be foolish to enter a negotiation without a clear idea of what I want to gain from it.

Some negotiations are simple, like determining the purchase price of a widget. Others, such as a labor dispute, may have dozens of considerations (e.g., payroll, insurance, advancement opportunities, tenure, leave options, office amenities, discounts, and many others). Each aspect to be negotiated can be measured in some way, and each party at the table has a goal for that aspect. We'll dig into that in a moment.

Considering Multiple Factors

Most inexperienced negotiators focus only on one aspect of a negotiation, to the exclusion of other factors that may be just as important. For instance, they may focus on price without considering other, non-monetary aspects like the strategic value of the relationship, the kind of ongoing support resources that will be involved, integration with other systems, and so forth.

Price is only one of many components of the Value portion of a negotiation, and it is by no means always the most important, but it is an easy one to focus on. As we saw in our chapter on strategy, expert negotiators look beyond the immediate issues, such as price, and look for ways to create mutually beneficial opportunities.

Price vs. Value

It is also important to remember that *price* and *value* are two distinctly different issues, in order to prepare successfully for your negotiations.

I recently received an email from a company that wanted to overhaul our website. These are smart people with expertise that I admire. But as I was looking over their packages, I noticed that the more expensive packages included several "bonus features" that held no interest for me.

This is a critical point to remember: value is entirely subjective. Price is a number you assign to an item based on the cost of production and profit margin, while value is a sense of the utility of something to you.

If I were to present a software package with a price tag of $30,000, and my competitor offered a package with a price tag of $20,000, you might be inclined to think my offer had a higher value. But if my software is challenging to operate or contains tools that don't align with your business, and their software is tailor-made for your industry and daily operations, then your perception would change: you would begin to see that my software has less value to you than my competitor's.

These concepts are essential to keep in mind as you consider the difference between your negotiation goals and your counterpart's, as well as your different perceptions of value.

Our next step is to identify a list of your objectives and your counterpart's objectives, including a view of each party's ideal outcome and each party's minimum acceptable level of agreement.

Set Your Aspiration Base—Your Ideal Outcome

In life, you will rarely get more than you ask for. It has been said that if you want to hit the moon, you should be aiming for the stars. Research has confirmed that high aspirations consistently outperform low ambitions. In negotiation, these high aspirations represent our best possible outcomes. We refer to our target for each objective as an "Aspiration Base," the goal to which we aspire.

If you are interviewing for a job, this would include things like your ideal (best possible) salary and benefits, choice of office, time off, and other negotiables. On the other hand, if you are the hiring manager, your Aspiration Base might be a lower starting salary and fewer perks.

If you have a good quality product/service/value proposition, there is no reason why you shouldn't have an ambitious Aspiration Base you can confidently present.

Having an Aspiration Base sets you up to "anchor" the negotiation, and it gives you some flexibility or room to move. Many professional negotiators measure their success by the concessions they can get from their counterparts. Your counterpart, at the same time, has no incentive to be flexible and to make a concession to you if you are not willing and able to make concessions to them (remember the rule of reciprocity). So, if you don't allow yourself some room to move away from your Aspiration Base in your counterpart's direction, you risk being seen as uncompromising and inflexible, and that can hurt the relationship right out of the starting gate.

When setting your Aspiration Base, remember:

- Always ask for more than you expect to get.

- Never accept your counterpart's first offer, always negotiate.

Set Your Real Base—Your Minimum Acceptable Outcome

Before you walk into any negotiation, you must be clear on your low threshold, the minimum acceptable outcome for you to agree. This may seem obvious, but in real life, your low threshold can be a moving target, particularly in a complex, multi-issue or multi-party negotiation, or in a situation where you have your heart (or your company's future) set on a specific outcome. If you don't know your bottom line, you risk selling yourself short. You can probably think of an occasion in your own life or career where you were so set on closing a deal (e.g., a job, a sale, a relationship) that you allowed yourself to be taken advantage of by your counterpart.

Returning to our job interview example, you must know the lowest salary level you are willing to accept, or you might end up with less than needed to pay your bills. Not having an identified Real Base is like going to the casino without having set yourself a limit at which you must stop gambling; you may find yourself losing badly as a consequence.

Also, consider what your counterpart's Real Base for the negotiation might be. If you are in the buying role, the seller across the table will have a minimum price they are willing to accept. If you are in the selling role, the buyer across from you might expect that you will offer additional benefits, like twenty-four-hour phone support or delivery on weekends. The more familiar you are with your counterpart's expectations, the better prepared you will be to offer concessions in exchange for some reciprocity from the other side.

You must keep clear on your objectives and values, as well as those of your counterpart (the checklist in Chapter 11 will help you to do this). You might be negotiating several factors at once (e.g., the price per unit, the number of units produced per month and the volume discount), where some elements have a higher Real Base and a lower Aspiration Base. At all times in your preparation and during the negotiations, keep yourself clear on your desired and acceptable outcomes, as well as those of your counterparts.

In doing so, you will observe something remarkable that can give you a significant advantage over your counterpart, especially if they haven't prepared as thoroughly as you.

Determine the Zone Of Possible Agreement (ZOPA)

Look carefully at this graphic, and you will find a powerful negotiation strategy hidden inside it.

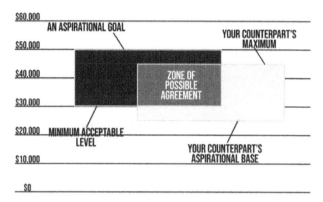

The Zone Of Possible Agreement (ZOPA) is the area between your Real Base and your counterpart's Real Base. During your preparations for negotiation, it is vital to establish whether there is a potential ZOPA and find a way to maximize it.

Let's say this graphic represents a salary negotiation between a new hire and a hiring manager. The new hire has established a minimum salary requirement of $30,000, while the hiring manager knows she has a cap of $45,000 for this position. That's good news because there is a Zone of Possible Agreement in that space. The negotiation can take place in that space, and both parties could likely come out feeling successful.

No ZOPA For You

Had those numbers been reversed (e.g., the new hire wanted at least $45,000, but the hiring manager had capped the position at $30,000), there would have been no ZOPA and the conversation would have ended without an agreement, unless the parties were able to create value in areas other than just the money. Or perhaps the new hire would have violated his Real Base and settled for a salary far below his needs, which I often see people do. You have probably witnessed this type of self-sacrifice as well. Sometimes, it is a wise negotiation strategy (accommodating), but unless it is part of a broader plan, it can really hurt you.

If you are hoping to reach an agreement and there is no identifiable ZOPA, you will have to get creative. You might need to invent opportunities for mutual gain. The more you know about your counterparts' needs, preferences, interests, and business model, the better positioned you are to find new ways to partner.

Let's say you are a startup wireless device manufacturer and you are trying to get a major telecom company to include your cellphones in their lineup. Their purchasing agent tells you that they are not accepting any new manufacturers' models for the foreseeable future, so there is no ZOPA. A creative option might be to suggest a partnership where you develop a unique wireless device and white-label it exclusively to this telecom, giving them the first position in a potential new market.

In those circumstances where there is no ZOPA and you are not able to invent new options for mutual gain, you will have to consider the alternatives to a negotiated agreement available to you and your counterparts. This is called a "BATNA."

Best Alternative To a Negotiated Agreement (BATNA)

The best source of power in any negotiation is the availability of alternatives. BATNA is short for "Best Alternative To A Negotiated Agreement." It is critical to investigate the BATNAs of all parties involved in the talks to gain a view of the relative positions of strength associated with each party.

Going back to our job interview situation, you are in a much better position if you have a few job offers available to you than you are if you have only one offer on the table.

Giving New Power To The Power Company

An example used to highlight the power of a BATNA is to look at a case study of what happened in the Electric Power Generation industry in Chile during the 1980s. There were three power companies with the ability to generate electricity in Chile, but only two of the three could distribute power to end users using a national grid infrastructure. Without this capability, the third company was forced to negotiate distribution capacity on the grid infrastructure of the other two players. Naturally, the two companies that owned their distribution systems ended up setting an exorbitant price for the third company.

The third company's problem was that they had no alternative distribution system; they had to use the distribution capacity of one of the other two companies.

The third company came up with a strategy to address this problem; they published a "Request For Proposal" to conduct a study of the feasibility of constructing a distribution network. The reaction in the market was immediate; within three months, they were able to negotiate a nearly twenty percent decrease in the cost of distribution.

It is startling to note that there wasn't even a real BATNA that led to this decrease; it was only the threat of creating an alternative that resulted in this movement. Interestingly, the study indicated that it was viable for a third company to build a distribution network, which they then eventually did.

Take It Or Leave It

You receive a significant boost in confidence when you walk into a negotiation knowing that you can take it or leave it. It is empowering to know that, no matter how the negotiation turns out, you are on solid ground. That is the power of the BATNA.

Many years ago, I bumped into an acquaintance who was clearly in distress. She was a new salesperson on a team and was preparing for a meeting with an important prospect.

When I asked, she said that this deal was the largest she had ever encountered and would be a significant win for the company, potentially one of the largest. The pressure of the outcome weighed heavily on her.

I tried getting her mind off the meeting, to no avail. Then I asked, "Does the company you're meeting with have competitors?"

"Of course," she replied.

I probed further: "Do you have contacts at any of those companies?"

She thought for a moment, then brightened, "I might have a couple of names."

"Great. Call them. You don't have to close a deal yet, just open a dialogue with them."

Why did I suggest that to her?

I knew that, as long as her subconscious mind kept open the possibility that another opportunity was in the offing, she would go into her next meeting with more confidence than if she went in believing her whole career hung on the outcome of that meeting.

Be Ready To Walk Away

No matter how intelligent or experienced you are, if you are what some sales professionals call "married to the outcome," you will go into the negotiation with pressure and anxiety. If you've ever spent any time in sales, you know that even the most poker-faced among us can transmit tension and stress through non-verbal communication if we feel that our well-being is dependent on a deal going a certain way. There is great power in being able to walk away from a deal.

The Case of Listeners vs. Tellers

Another common mistake negotiators make is that they come to the negotiation table prepared to talk about themselves, but with no clue (and often no interest) in what the other party needs. If you are engaging a competitive strategy and don't care if you ever see the party across the table from you again, then this is a legitimate approach. But if you are looking for a long-term, mutually beneficial relationship with your counterpart, it is a crippling failure.

This is a consistent pattern we see when we observe individuals in negotiations (and frankly, in everyday life): people have a tendency to share their point of view rather than inquire first about their counterpart's point of view. In doing so, they leave more than money on the table; they miss out on massive opportunities to partner creatively and synergistically. We do it at home, too, and the missed opportunities can be just as significant. The best listeners make the best spouses, the best parents, the best bosses, the best teachers, the best clergy, and the best neighbors.

If you want to be successful in any area of life (but particularly as a negotiator), you must be willing and able to ask meaningful questions and listen carefully to the responses. Failing to ask questions is a failure of preparation, and it exposes your interests without learning anything about your counterpart's interests.

Preparation

If you have done a thorough job preparing for a negotiation, you already know some things about your counterparts' needs, interests, positions, and priorities, but more importantly, you know what you don't know. Once you identify the information you are missing, you know what questions you need to ask. A smart negotiator enters the meeting not with a list of demands but a list of questions to ask his counterpart. Asking questions brings out needs, interests, and priorities you couldn't have known any other way. The negotiator who does all the telling and none of the asking is sinking his own ship, and minimizing the opportunity.

It is fair to say that while you are talking, you are certainly not learning anything from anyone else. One of the critical skills that will be sure to improve your negotiation outcomes is the skill of questioning. You are very unlikely to be asking too many questions.

On the other hand, making assumptions is one of the most dangerous things you can do in the context of negotiation. Clearly, you must make some assumptions as you prepare, but those assumptions should show you what questions you need to be asking during the negotiation. Your questioning serves to validate or invalidate your premises so you can move past them into the truth of the situation. More than that, it brings out information that can lead you to greater partnership opportunities, or show you when to walk away.

Execution

Failure to ask essential questions not only cuts you off from much-needed information, but it also dishonors your counterpart. It demonstrates that you don't care one whit about their needs, interests, and values. Again, if you genuinely don't care about the relationship and you only ever embrace a competitive strategy, then talk away. The Rule of Reciprocity will exact its judgment on you later.

Listening well is an entry-level people skill. I'm not referring to listening with the intent to respond, but rather, listening with the intent to understand what the other person is saying. This is a matter of personal development, and frankly, most people lack it. Human nature is inherently selfish and self-serving. The most successful people are those who have moved past human nature and developed the habit of listening to others.

Listening to others values them, but it also gives you value. We tend to trust people when we feel they are hearing us. We feel valued and valuable. This is not soft, feel-good blather; this is how humans operate. If you want to be successful as a negotiator, you must create trust and build rapport. Listening with the intent to understand and honor the person across from you is the foundation to the relationship.

Deal Objective Checklist

As we conclude this chapter, I want to offer a short checklist to help you be sure you haven't left out something important from your preparations.

1. Identify all the issues you and your counterpart want to discuss and the objectives you want to achieve during this round of negotiation. Prioritize all the objectives.

2. Establish the value of the terms to be discussed before you negotiate on price. Sometimes, price isn't an important decision criterion.

3. For every single objective, establish:

    a. Your Aspiration Base—an ideal outcome

    b. Your counterpart's Aspiration Base (to the best of your knowledge—validate your assumptions at the negotiation)

    c. Your Real Base—your minimum acceptable outcome

    d. Your counterpart's Real Base (again, draw from available information or confirm your assumptions when you meet with them)

5. If necessary, develop different options to satisfy your counterpart's interests. You may need some creativity to find opportunities where there appears to be none.

6. Identify which of your objectives you share with your counterpart and which ones may be in conflict with your counterpart's. Again, think outside the box and look for creative options.

7. Identify (or develop) alternatives to the deal (BATNA). The better your BATNA, the more confidence you have going into the negotiation. Do the same from your counterpart's perspective.

8. Look for gaps in your information and assumptions you've made and develop questions to fill in missing information and validate your assumptions. Consider finding ways to partner beyond what is on the agenda and prepare questions to set up those conversations.

Sample Questions:

- "I understand that you would like to discuss price, marketing spend, volume, and length of the contract. Is there anything else that you would like to talk about?"

- "OK, now that I have a clear understanding of all the issues, can you help me to organize them in terms of issues most and least important to you? They are probably all important, but if you had to prioritize them, how would you do that?"

- "I see that price, marketing budget and volume discounts are important issues to you. Of these items, which do you consider to be deal breakers?'

Key Takeaways from Chapter Six

- In the Value pillar of negotiation, we measurably quantify the goals and objectives for both parties in a specific negotiation.

- It is crucial to be clear on your objectives before entering any negotiation, including your Aspiration Base and your Real Base.

- Value is subjective.

- The more accurately you can identify your counterpart's goals, objectives, and values, the better prepared you will be to develop the Zone for Possible Agreement.

- While you must make some assumptions about your counterpart during your preparations, carefully-prepared questions will serve to validate or invalidate your assumptions before you act on them.

- Sometimes, you may have to walk away from a negotiation without a deal. The more alternatives you have going in, the less pressure you will be under to accept a suboptimal deal. Remember that no deal is better than a bad deal.

> *"Accepting that people perceive value differently—and that value has no right or wrong angles—will help you to be less emotionally tied to your position, and more exploratory of your counterparts' needs."*

—Jan Potgieter

Apply It To Your Situation

1. Identify three things you learned from this chapter that you want to begin implementing in your negotiations. Highlight the one you want to do first.

_____

_____

_____

_____

2. Describe ways that your previous negotiations have benefitted from your clear understanding of your counterpart or suffered from false assumptions.

_____

_____

_____

_____

3. Describe an area of your life where you would like to see more accurate and thorough preparation in operation.

_____

_____

_____

_____

4. What did you learn about negotiation in this chapter that surprised or enlightened you?

_____

_____

_____

_____

Chapter Seven: Concessions

Executive Summary

- You make decisions on emotion more than facts, even if you think you are basing your decisions on facts.

- Trying to convince your counterpart of your position with evidence will only provoke them to respond with opposing evidence, and you will most likely hit a stalemate.

- By leaving room for concessions, you leverage the Rule of Reciprocity to work for you instead of against you.

- Anchoring is a powerful way to set a benchmark against which every other position will be measured.

- If your counterpart sets an anchor that is not favorable to you, there are ways to re-anchor in your favor.

- Power is not always what we think it is, and our perceptions dictate how we respond.

The Truth Behind The Decisions We Make

Contrary to popular belief, decision making is not a strictly rational process, no matter how stoic and logical we may consider ourselves to be. As humans, we make decisions through a multipart system that includes the facts of the situation (or at least our perception of those facts) and how we feel about those facts.

In fact, unless you are a Vulcan from Star Trek and incapable of emotion, you consistently make decisions with emotions, and then attempt justify those decisions with logic and facts. If we are honest with ourselves, we must admit that we use feelings to select and prioritize the facts we consider in any decision.

Previously, we have referred to this as Confirmation Bias—giving preference to facts that support the decisions our emotions have already made. Your choice of which news agencies you trust should be proof enough of that.

Let me ask you a question: what is the universal standard of fairness?

Is there such a thing? No, of course not. Value, as we saw in Chapter 6, is strictly subjective and we base our judgment on how we feel about the item. Price is an attempt to assign an objective means of measurement, but we judge whether the item is worth the stated price subjectively. Trust is an emotion. It may be based on the facts of history, or it may not be. Those facts may be clouded by the feelings you experienced at the time the event occurred, or by the feelings you are experiencing at this moment, or by the perspective that you hold. Emotions can distort everything; they can also clarify things for you.

What Is More Important?

Imagine for a moment that there is a fence between your house and your neighbor's, and you woke up one morning to find it damaged. The repairs will be expensive, but it's not clear who is responsible for the cost.

Let's say you grew up in a military family, being stationed all over the world and moved to a new location every two years. You wouldn't have had an opportunity to form long-term relationships with your neighbors. So, what would be more important to you in this dispute—the money or the relationship? Likely, you would be more concerned about the money.

Now, let's say that you grew up in a neighborhood where your family lived for twenty-five or thirty years and built long-term friendships with the neighbors. Wouldn't you be more likely to prioritize the relationship with the neighbor over the cost of the repairs?

Don't hear what I'm not saying. I'm not saying once-off relationships are deserving of a competitive, low effort approach. All relationships are important.

Your perspective on what is important, fair, and acceptable is influenced by, among other things, the way you were raised, your religion, your culture, your family values, your profession, and a host of other factors. What is acceptable behavior to one person may very well be utterly unacceptable behavior to another. Who's to say what is important and what is not? What is far more important than being right is understanding what your counterparts think and value so that you set yourself up to be able to serve their needs, rather than just serving your own.

Leading With The Evidence

Consider the implications of this. When you make a case based solely on the evidence available to you at the moment, you open a minefield, because you presume to have rational judgment. The fact is, you are building on sandy ground.

I am often intrigued by the negotiation research that comes out of academic institutions. For instance, in one study, they got a group of senior executives together and gave them all a set of financial statements. Then they split the room in half and said, "Team A is going to prepare to sell this business, and Team B is going to prepare to buy this business. Now, go create a valuation for the business based on the financial statements." Guess who values the business to be worth more and guess who values it to be worth less?

There are no surprises to be found here: the buyers value the company to be worth less, and the sellers estimate it to be worth more. Because we naturally look for the evidence to confirm our perspectives, both groups can look at the same data but come to different conclusions about value. Sometimes wildly different outcomes.

Here again, we see Confirmation Bias at work.

It is natural for us to look for and find only the evidence that supports our case. In reality, there is almost no such thing as an objective perspective that is 100% rational. All of us make decisions emotionally and use convenient facts to back up the decision we've made. Have you or someone you know ever bought a brand new car they couldn't really afford and then spent the rest of the day justifying it to themselves and everyone else?

Our western education system is stacked toward building an argument by leading with evidence Unfortunately, leading with evidence doesn't help us solve the people problem. People have their own opinions and perceptions, and each of us has an ego that puts our needs, desires, and values ahead of anything else. Using the evidence to prove that you are right (and your counterpart is wrong) almost always puts the other person on the defensive and conditions them to resist what you are saying. You provoke objections and pushback from the very person you are trying to win over. The Rule of Reciprocity is alive and well—when you lead with the evidence, you can expect your counterpart to respond with their proof that supports their perspective (otherwise known as objections).

Against this backdrop, it is tough for me to understand why some of the world's leading universities would advise negotiators to use so-called "objective criteria" to support the way they present their arguments. The fact is that there is no such thing as "objective criteria" that can be universally applied. Sure, there may be some cases where two parties might agree to reference the same "objective" third-party source in support of finding agreement. However, if there really were something like objective criteria embraced by all people, we wouldn't have to go to court to settle any disputes, we would just reference the universally-accepted criteria. Can you see how futile the notion of using "objective criteria" to support your negotiations really is?

I'm not suggesting that you should ever run the risk of not having solid evidence to support your recommendations and arguments; just don't lead with it. Lead with relationship.

Harness Reciprocity to Win

Interestingly, negotiation research has confirmed that the number one contributor to deal satisfaction is receiving concessions from your counterpart. That's right, not hitting your target or getting everything you asked for, but getting your counterpart to move in your direction by making concessions to you is what brings satisfaction to all parties. By being cooperative and moving in your direction, your counterpart is signaling that you and your interests hold significance and importance to them to the extent that they are willing to give up some of their desires to meet yours. Isn't that how coupons and twenty percent-off sales work? You feel like you are getting something extra from the retailer.

So, when you make concessions, you send a strong signal that you recognize and understand your counterpart's interests and that you are prepared to move in their direction to satisfy those interests. In turn, this means that your counterpart will be significantly more likely to reciprocate by making concessions in your direction. Just as evidence will attract objections and counter-evidence, concessions will attract counter-concessions.

The Power of Human Nature

What I'm pointing out to you is fundamental to human nature. The irony is that it is far easier to leverage what we know about human nature to move toward agreement than it is to convince your counterpart that your argument and supporting evidence are correct. For your counterpart to agree that your evidence and reasoning are right means that they might have to sacrifice some of their credibility by admitting that their evidence is incorrect. Who likes to do that?

There are compelling considerations that I want to bring out of this that will help you to harness and exploit the power of human nature to significantly increase the likelihood of achieving your objectives.

Anchoring

As we've discovered, human nature tends to make us want to go to the evidence to prove our point. But, surprisingly, our opinions are not so much influenced by the veracity and validity of the evidence, but much more just by whatever happened first. You may have heard about the importance of first impressions and how they leave a lasting imprint on us. Well, when it comes to negotiating, first impressions are important.

It is critical to your negotiation strategy and preparation that you embrace this: the way that you will have the most control and influence in your negotiations is by managing the frame of the negotiation. This starts with something we call anchoring.

Let's consider an example I often use in our advanced negotiation seminars.

All participants in our advanced negotiation seminars participate in at least one filmed negotiation simulation with a professional negotiator. The brief we use for this simulation is designed to bring to life some of the key strategies, tactics, and techniques that you're reading about in this book. Sometimes we provide the participants with a brief where we task them to agree on a price reduction of five percent on the renewal of a contract with an incumbent vendor (played by a professional negotiator).

We tell them in the brief that the vendor has requested a ten percent increase in price and that the vendor has a lot of power (more power than the buyer) as they are the only provider of a software solution that is essential for the business represented by the participant. Then, when we start the negotiation, the professional negotiator (the vendor) ensures that they bring up the topic of price first. They share with the participant that the price has actually increased by twenty-three percent, not ten percent, and that they've actually swallowed thirteen percent of the twenty-three percent increase to only pass on ten percent to the buyer, as if they've done them a favor.

There is an excellent reason why we approach the negotiation this way. By making the first mention of the price (effectively making the first offer in this case), we create an anchor in the mind of our counterpart around a number that is even higher than what they expected when they came into the exercise. What typically happens is that they would have prepared a request for a price reduction in the region of ten or perhaps even fifteen percent so that they leave themselves some room to end up with the five percent reduction that their brief instructs them to pursue.

But, because we outline that the price actually went up by twenty-three percent, and we already supposedly "swallowed" thirteen percent of the price increase, the participants start negotiating with themselves. They start lowering their aspirations and instead of asking for a ten or fifteen percent reduction in the price, they now typically ask for only the five percent reduction just because we managed to "anchor" their perspective around our view of the price rather than theirs. We make the conversation about the twenty-three percent "actual" increase and our expectation for a minimum of a ten percent increase from them.

We do everything we can to take away the focus from their expectations and their desire to obtain a five percent decrease in the price. All of this through managing the "frame" or perspective of the negotiation by creating an "anchor" or reference point around our expectations, rather than our counterpart's. Because our anchor is highly ambitious, not only does this approach allow us to control the frame of the negotiation, it also creates room for us to satisfy our counterpart by making concessions as the exercise progresses.

Using ambitious reference points or anchors throughout the negotiation is the hallmark of elite level negotiators. Elite level negotiators are also masters at re-anchoring any anchors thrown out by their counterparts. Every once in a while we come across a participant who manages to re-anchor the numbers we throw out in this exercise, and they usually are experienced negotiators. But this happens very rarely (less than five percent of the time), which serves to underline the power of successfully harnessing this technique.

Concessions

In a practical sense, the most significant sign that my counterpart is interested in me and is open to seeing the deal from my perspective is when she makes a concession. A concession is made when one party moves from its initial position to a more moderate position. When you move in my direction by accepting less than your original request, you are signaling an effort to meet me halfway. All humans desire significance. We want to know that we matter, that we are important, and that people consider our opinion.

So how do you demonstrate to somebody that you care? By telling them about yourself and the strength and the validity of your case? No, of course not. You demonstrate their significance to you by saying, "I'm moving in your direction. I give recognition to you and your needs."

But this point is critical: you can only do that if you've left yourself room to make a concession.

There Is A Wrong Way To Make A Concession

When making concessions, it is very important that you present it the right way, otherwise they may not be recognized as a concession by your counterpart at all. Let's say that you have been invited to submit a proposal for your widgets to a very big and powerful company. You are aware that there will probably be a lot of your competitors also bidding for this contract. So, as you sit and discuss the opportunity with your team, you decide that instead of your normal list price of $100 per widget, you will be submitting your proposal at a price of $88 per widget.

Now, put yourself in your counterpart's shoes for a moment (the buyer for the big and powerful company receiving your offer). Does she know that you made a concession by discounting your normal list price from $100 to $88, or does she believe that your normal price is $88? Unless you've clearly made it known in your proposal that your normal price is $100 and you have made a concession (by clearly indicating the level of discount you're offering), your counterpart will not recognize that you've made a concession and therefore will not feel any inclination to reciprocate according to the Rule of Reciprocity.

Making concessions is most impactful when you can do it in the moment, face-to-face with your counterpart. When your counterpart objects to your price and you go away for a couple of days and return with an updated proposal, your counterpart is more likely to interpret that as a new proposal than a concession. It is far more powerful to ensure that you are thoroughly prepared to be able to make concessions in the moment.

If your counterpart says to you: "I'm sorry, but $100 is more than we have budgeted for and also more than any of your competitors are asking," you should respond by making a concession in the moment: "If we are able to get a deal closed by the end of

the week I would be able to discount the price by nine percent, from $100 to $91."
This makes it clear to your counterpart that you are indeed offering a concession (in
this case, a conditional concession based on getting the deal done quickly).

Leaving Room For Concessions

This is central to your negotiation success, yet I see people mess it up every day.

Like all people, you might often negotiate with yourself rather than with your
counterpart. What do I mean by that?

Let's say you sell a widget for which you absolutely need to receive $100, so you ask
for $100 because you want to get a deal done quickly. Then your counterpart comes
back and says, "No, we can't do $100; we can only do $80." Now, you're forced to go
back to the evidence of why they must give you $100 because you haven't left yourself
room to make a concession.

Think of the Rule of Reciprocity. What will you have coming back at you? They
are going to find the evidence to support their case for $80, where it would have
been much easier if you had simply asked for a little more than $100 and made a
concession, or even better, several concessions. What reciprocity would that most
likely have provoked? A counter-concession. You make a move toward their side,
so they make a move toward your side. You are getting closer because you are both
choosing to get closer together. Even though this is not an exact science, it harnesses
human nature rather than evidence to create momentum towards agreement.

Smart people have a tough time with this. I promise you; the more intelligent
people are, the harder it is for them to grasp this because they often want to dispense
with what they consider the "soft skills" and focus on getting what they want using
reason and evidence.

The first time I took my now-wife, Linda, on a date, we were negotiating. Now, it
didn't sound like the talk you might hear in a contract dispute, but we were asking
questions back and forth to see if a relationship was desirable. If I had spent the date
telling her about my qualifications, my degrees, my bank accounts, and so forth,
it would have ended badly. But this is precisely what so many of us do when we
negotiate.

What did I do instead? I explored her interests and found common ground. I
wasn't pitching an idea or a product. You should identify what is essential to your
counterpart and then connect what you have to what's important to them. That's
how it works best. Whether you're selling a product, interviewing a job candidate,
or considering a life partner, you need to identify what matters to them and then
connect your offering to their needs.

It is tempting to bypass this and focus on making an argument with facts and
reasoning. Let's say in the dating scenario above, I felt certain that it was inevitable
that Linda and I would be getting married. If I said to her on the first date: "We've
got this relationship thing down, so let's stop all this dating nonsense and just get

married." Would that have worked? Of course not. There may be some exceptions to the rule, but I'll tell you that this approach would be very high risk. You must go through the courting process before you can get married or you are in for a rocky road. It works the same way in negotiation. When you think, "The facts are clearly in favor of my position, so the discussion is over," you open yourself up to objection and rejection. You must take people on the journey toward your position in a way that honors their perspective, even if you think their perspective is foolish. The evidence alone will rarely get them there.

What is the journey I'm talking about?

You must create satisfaction by initiating an exchange; you make a concession to move toward them, and they reciprocate by exchanging a concession of their own. Concessions cultivate a productive climate.

This approach may seem counterintuitive, but it aligns with human nature. Have you ever noticed that when your counterpart accepts your first offer with no pushback, neither party is ultimately satisfied? Why is that? Because it hasn't felt like a journey.

It was too easy.

Let's Buy A House In England

In England, when you buy and sell a house, it's different than just about anywhere else in the world. In most countries, the offer made by the buyer is binding. In places like the United States, Australia, Germany—in fact, in most nations—if you make an offer for a house, you must live up to that offer. If it were accepted, then that deal is enforced. But in England, you have to physically exchange contracts or the deal is not done.

Let's say I make an offer for £ 500,000 on a house in London, and the owner accepts it. If I were to go and sell my house—because now I'm going to move into her home—she could still come back to me in the days before we're due to exchange contracts and say, "Sorry, the deal is off because I got a better deal." But now, I've already sold my house, and I have nowhere to stay because the deal to buy the new house has fallen through. When this happens in England, the locals will say that you've been "gazumped."

Real Estate agents in England will tell you that you are far more likely to be gazumped if the first offer to buy a house was accepted by the seller. Why? Because the seller now thinks they can get a better deal if it was so easy to get an offer at or close to their list price.

The Time The Bank Said Yes

To give you another practical example, some years ago, I presented an offer to roll out a negotiation skills development program to a large investment bank. They had a committee of seven people, and after I presented, they asked me, "Would you mind waiting outside for ten minutes?" I figured they wanted to talk through some additional questions, and I would hear from them in a week or a month after they had a chance to do their due diligence. Instead, they called me back in and said, "Let's do it. When can we start?"

Now, mind you, I had marked up my price by thirty percent over the list price. It was the first time I had pursued work with an investment bank. I was confident they were going to try to drive a hard bargain (see my false assumption?), so I needed to make sure I left some room in the deal to be able to make some concessions. But then, they just flat-out accepted my first offer. I was going to get thirty percent more than I expected as a result, but I'll never forget the first thing I did. I called Linda and said, "I can't believe that they accepted my first offer. And at a rate that is significantly higher than our usual rates! Perhaps we should be asking significantly more for our services." My first response was that I realized I was undervaluing my service. They were used to paying much more.

You never want to accept the first offer because it doesn't create satisfaction. Remember, It's the fact that I move in your direction that creates satisfaction.

The Anchor Sticks Unless You Move It

So, what happened here? Let's return to the concept of anchoring: whatever happens first creates a reference point or an anchor. Sometimes the anchor sticks and sometimes you can re-anchor it.

In this case with the bank, my anchor stuck, and I was surprised by it.

Usually, what we see is that the strike price (or final accepted offer) lies closest to the initial anchor, no matter how many other counteroffers come up, but there is usually some movement first.

When you study the list of tactics in Chapter Five, you'll see one called "The Extreme Offer." Now I'm not suggesting you should be extreme in your expectations when it comes to anchoring, but there is a lesson about anchoring to be learned from extreme offers because they can create an environment where your counterpart is able to "save face." In some cultures, like in Asia and the Middle East, the extreme offer tactic can be used without fear of negotiations turning personal and defensive because of the premium associated with allowing people to retain their dignity and credibility, or "save face." In these cultures, you will often hear heated debate, but the contents of the discussions are rarely personal.

Contrast the traditional Middle Eastern & Asian markets with the typical Western style of negotiating. In the West, we generally don't feel any obligation to let people save face or retain their dignity. In the West we typically are more inclined to get personal in our arguments and cause our counterparts to "lose face" or sacrifice their credibility.

Following a Western style of negotiating, if you came to me with a ridiculous extreme offer based on me expressing interest to buy a widget that I believe to be worth $10 against your belief that it should be worth $50, my argument with the you might sound something like this: "Well, you know what? That's insane. Clearly you don't understand the market. I've done the supply chain analysis of this gadget, and we've looked at the composition of all the input materials. Our view is that it's worth no more than $10." This is an example of leading with evidence to support my position.

Then you (as my Western counterpart) will probably say, "You clearly didn't look at the supply chain analysis the right way. This gadget is definitely worth $50. Is it not merely the sum of its parts, but it is also the result of years' worth of research and other input costs over and above the raw materials that went into manufacturing the product. Lastly, we also know that the components of the material are a little bit different from what you thought."

Can you see how it's so easy to get locked in the evidence game? You had to reciprocate with evidence because I led with it, instead of giving you room to save face.

Now, by contrast, let's consider the Middle Eastern & Asian market negotiation or haggling style: the salesman says he wants $50 for the gadget. So, you respond: "You know what? My grandmother used to look after our kids so that my wife could work. Unfortunately, she died recently, and now my wife has had to give up her job because she must take care of our kids, and that's why I can only offer you $2.00." This tactic is called "The Emotional Appeal."

That now creates space for your counterpart to concede and move in your direction because he's not bound by reciprocity to defend his evidence. He might then say, "Oh, if that's the case then, of course, I can help you out. Let's call it $25." It doesn't become personal.

The moment you make it personal, you've got a problem, because you are not only attacking your counterpart's position, you are attacking her character. You set yourself up for pushback and objections because you provoke them by not giving your counterpart room to save face and make concessions. It is important that you create space for your counterpart to be able to move in your direction. Your arguments and supporting evidence only serve to paint your counterpart into a corner, and reduces the likelihood that they will move in your direction, because for them to do so will come at the expense of their credibility.

What Came First?

As you can see, what happens first is critical in any negotiation. As you develop your skills, you can start to build some of these best practices into how you frame your offers. For example: "Normally, in a case like this, I'd be expecting a price of $140,000, but in light of the unique opportunity offered by this potential partnership, I'm going to ask you for only $132,000."

What have I already done in my opening offer? I've already conceded to you so now I'm setting myself up to harness reciprocity. If I want this negotiation to be characterized by concessions, then I need to lead by offering concessions.

Most people don't get this. Traditional negotiation training emphasizes that you should always ask for something in return when you make a concession. But when you do this, you are going against human nature because, of course, your counterpart won't see that as a concession at all.

They will merely interpret it as a conditional offer, not a concession. Making concessions in a way that will engage the Rule of Reciprocity is a learned skill, which is why it is so important that you practice your negotiation skills by participating in negotiation simulations.

Once you have mastered the skill of making concessions the right way, you can connect it to making counter-concessions or counter-trades. But the way most people teach negotiation includes making conditional offers cloaked as concessions. This completely misses out on harnessing the power of reciprocity, because your counterpart feels they are being pushed into giving up something. You only engage reciprocity when your counterpart recognizes your concessions as real and sincere, not conditional.

When I share this information in our seminars, I regularly have people ask me if this is not just manipulation, so let me pause for a minute and give you my perspective.

What Is Manipulation?

The word *manipulation* is poorly understood. When we use the word, it usually carries negative connotations. Yet, the dictionary definition of manipulation has several potential applications, including "to manage or utilize skillfully." Consider for a moment whether you think it would be a bad thing if we could positively manipulate smokers to quit smoking? Or if we could positively manipulate drivers always to obey the speed limit and wear their safety belts? Wouldn't these be great examples of cases where we would be happy to bring some manipulation to bear on the results we desire?

When we started this book, we spoke about the characteristics of success, and we learned that it is essential to have heightened ambition to attain exceptional results. So, one way of looking at this is to be ambitious in your expectations so that you can still allow yourself to make concessions—it has nothing to do with being negatively manipulative. Instead, it is positively manipulative to create an atmosphere or climate within which the likelihood of reaching an agreement will be significantly enhanced.

Letting People Say "No"

It takes courage to let people say "no" to you. Most people don't like hearing "no" from their counterparts, but there is an opportunity hidden in every "no" you receive. In a negotiation, it's okay if people say "no" to you, because then you can create new opportunities to satisfy them by making concessions...if you have left yourself room to do so. Plus, your concessions are likely to provoke counter-concessions, which sets you on the path to an agreement.

If you are unwilling to accept a "no" from your counterpart, then the idea of anchoring your offer to a high Aspiration Base and making concessions to move toward their position will be difficult for you to handle, and you will not enjoy significant success as a negotiator. You will cut yourself off from some spectacular deals and strong business relationships, because you won't be able to give your counterpart the satisfaction of receiving concessions. You must be able to separate your value as a person from your counterpart's valuation of your offer. That's a matter of personal development.

What I'm not saying is that you should necessarily be extreme in your demands, at least in the Western world. If you want $100, you might ask for $105. The extreme demand—where you ask for $200 when you want $100—is standard operating procedure in the Middle East, India, China, but not here. It's just part of the culture of negotiating in those parts of the world. As long as you are negotiating in the Western world, by all means anchor your position higher than you need, but with more moderation.

Making The First Offer

Now on to the million-dollar question, the question that invariably comes up at this point in my live events: who should make the first offer?

If you survey the negotiation skills development space, you will find several different answers to this question. Some "experts" will say that you should *never* make the first offer; you should *always* let your counterpart make the first offer. Other "experts" will recommend that you should be the one always making the first offer. There there are those who say that it depends on the situation.

So, what is the right approach? Cue our golfer.

In my opinion, if you want to be an exceptional negotiator, you must understand how to evaluate who should make the first offer in each negotiation setting. This particular issue is so often misunderstood—even by the so-called "experts" who teach negotiation skills—that it is seldom used to its full effect. Once you understand the rationale behind it, it will have a powerful impact on your results as a negotiator.

In business, the seller generally makes the first offer. When you walk into a store, the products are all labeled with prices. When a buyer calls for proposals, the sellers come back with their pricing. But that is not always the case. Most job listings include a salary range the employer is willing to pay. That is as much a negotiation as a purchasing deal. Similarly, if a professional buyer is using a highly-assertive approach, they might come to the table with an established target price they are willing to pay. If you are the seller in that situation, you won't get the opportunity to make the first offer. It is important to note that negotiations are not purely buyer/seller scenarios, which is why it so important to understand the dynamics of each unique encounter.

The key here is the same as in every other aspect of negotiation: you must be able to read the signals and adjust your game plan to fit the conditions. Sometimes, you will get to make the first offer and sometimes you won't. Be prepared for it to go either way. In golfing terms, have a wood and an iron handy.

I want to take your behind the scenes of a negotiation so you can find a clue as to who should make the first offer.

Who Has The Power In This Negotiation?

Let's say that Charles is working in a job where he is paid $30,000 per year and he has applied for a different job that offers to pay between $40,000 and $50,000, depending on experience and qualifications. Let's go behind the scenes to Charles' house the night before the negotiation and look for clues about who has the power. Charles is sitting with his wife and a close friend, discussing his approach to his upcoming interview. The conversation might sound like this:

"I'd love to ask for $50,000. That's almost double what I'm earning now. But I've heard that there will be a lot of people interviewing for this role. I should probably come in at $45,000. I could even come in at $40,000; that would probably make me very competitive. You know, worst case scenario, I could sneak in even lower—under $40,000. Most of the other guys are going to be asking for closer to $50,000. Coming in really low would position me well and it's still more than what I'm earning now."

What is Charles doing in this example? You've guessed it; he is negotiating with himself before he ever gets to the interview. Can you identify with this scenario? Have you ever negotiated with yourself? We have all done it.

Why is it so easy to fall into the trap of negotiating with ourselves?

The reason you lower your expectations—a.k.a. negotiating with yourself—is because of your view of the relative position of power. You think that the employing organization has more power than you (there are many other people interviewing for the position, so they have the advantage of alternatives). When we believe that we don't have the good cards in our hand, we tend to lower our expectations.

Perceptions of Power

This means that you need to be aware of your relative position of power, but you must also recognize that your perception of your relative position of power may not be equal with reality. To say it another way, your perception of your relative position of power has more impact on how you negotiate than your true position.

If my counterpart has the perception that he has more power than me (because he has many other alternatives to choose from), he is likely going to be more demanding. Conversely, if his perception is that he doesn't have the power in our relationship (because I am the only vendor with the tools or expertise he needs), he will likely be less demanding.

So, If I have greater relative power than my counterpart, and we both know it, who should make the first offer? In this case, I should let my counterpart make the first offer because chances are, he's going to come to that meeting having already negotiated with himself, perhaps lowering his Aspiration Base, and maybe even lowering his Real Base. He's probably going to come up with something better than I would have expected. It doesn't matter if you're buying or selling. If you're buying, you can easily make a first offer by indicating a target price or budget to your counterpart.

What about the case where it is unclear where the power balance lies? For instance, in a situation where we believe that there is parity in power between us and our counterpart? In this case, I would recommend that you go ahead and make the first offer because of the powerful effect of anchoring and making the negotiation about your aspirational objectives, rather than your counterpart's. That could tip the scales in your favor for the rest of the meeting.

It is probably fair to say that you should attempt to make the first offer around eighty percent of the time. But you should ask yourself each time you negotiate where the power balance lies and, more importantly, where everyone at the table believes the power balance lies. Perceptions drive decisions. Also remember that if you feel like you don't have much power and that your counterpart holds all the advantages, you are likely to negotiate with yourself and lower your aspirations. In this case, make sure that you remain ambitious and leave yourself room to make concessions down the line. Stick to your aspirations, even if they feel too ambitious at first, and don't allow the negotiations to start at the level of your Real Base.

It sounds noble to humble yourself before a person of greater perceived power, but it takes away your ability to make concessions with ease, and thereby, to create a high level of satisfaction for your counterpart. Remember how we said that people derive more satisfaction from a negotiation where the two parties came to an agreement through trading concessions than one where they got everything they wanted right out of the gate? By negotiating yourself down to a lower aspiration, you steal that satisfaction from them, as well as block yourself from possibly achieving more than you thought possible. Everyone loses in the end.

So, you are better off risking a more ambitious approach and giving them room to say "no." Then you can create satisfaction by making concessions. If you are in a situation where your counterpart has numerous options to choose from and you do not, you may want to be more accommodating, but you must not give up the ship before the first volley is fired.

Again, whatever happens first is key to setting the tone for the rest of the negotiation and anchoring the numbers you want in your counterpart's mind.

This is pivotal.

If you think you don't have the power, you must force yourself to be more ambitious. Whatever you were thinking, you need to be more demanding. If you have the power and both parties know it, you should let them make the first offer. If they anchor the price in a range that doesn't suit you, there are ways to re-anchor it later.

Key Takeaways from Chapter Seven

- Humans make decisions based on emotions and use logic and facts to support those decisions later. We use Confirmation Bias to filter out facts that conflict with our decisions.

- Whether you lead with evidence that supports your position or with valuing the relationship over your position, the Rule of Reciprocity will compel your counterpart to respond in kind, so choose wisely.

- The Law of First Impressions states that whatever information is presented first creates an "anchor" in the minds of everyone at the table by which all other information is evaluated. Whoever makes the first offer typically sets the anchor for the negotiation.

- It is possible to re-anchor the discussion with new information.

- When you anchor your position higher than you hope to receive, it gives you room to move in your counterparts' direction by making concessions. Making concessions allows you to leverage the Rule of Reciprocity to draw your counterparts toward your position without making them feel that you're taking advantage of them.

- When two parties make concessions in a negotiation, both parties usually feel a higher sense of satisfaction from the encounter than when one party accepts the first offer.

- You must present your concessions in a tangible way or the other party will not recognize that you have made them, and will not feel obligated to reciprocate.

- In most negotiations, one party is in a position of greater power than the other, either because they have many alternatives to choose from or some other advantage, but the position of power might also be an illusion held by one or both parties. If one party believes the other has the position of power, they will usually act accordingly, in effect giving the other party power.

"Power is of two kinds. One is obtained by the fear of punishment and the other by acts of love. Power based on love is a thousand times more effective and permanent then the one derived from fear of punishment.."

—Mahatma Gandhi

Apply It To Your Situation

1. Identify three things you learned from this chapter that you want to begin implementing in your daily life. Highlight the one you want to do first.

   _____

   _____

   _____

2. Describe how you see the Rule of Reciprocity operating in your life. Are you using it to your advantage or disadvantage?

   _____

   _____

   _____

3. What will you do differently in your next negotiation knowing what you now know about anchoring?

   _____

   _____

   _____

4. Describe a situation where you would benefit from more effective use of concessions.

   _____

   _____

   _____

5. What is power? Where do you have power and where does someone else have power over you?

   _____

   _____

   _____

6. What did you learn about negotiation in this chapter that surprised or enlightened you?

   _____

   _____

   _____

Chapter Eight: Controlling the Negotiation

Executive Summary

- Framing is a powerful tool for establishing a common understanding of the objectives and parameters of the negotiation.

- You can frame the negotiation in terms of what you and your counterpart stand to gain or lose, depending on the outcome.

- Once a frame has been set, it is possible to reframe the conversation in a way that puts your position in a more favorable light.

- Asking questions is an effective way to reframe, uncover information, identify your counterparts' values, interests, preferences, objectives, and strategy. You can also use questions to identify and address objections.

- Use questions effectively in all four pillars of the negotiation.

Pillar 3: Process

At this point, we will move from Pillar 2 (Value) onto the third pillar (Process), which is where structuring the approach to deal making comes in.

Framing the Negotiation

While there is no official or linear process to a negotiation, the application of a few powerful tools will help you gain and maintain control of the conversation. Framing and reframing is the art of managing both content and perceptions and ensures that your issues and perspectives will get time and attention. Whatever you say when you initiate talks creates context and expectations for the discussion, and impacts how your counterparts perceive the situation or an issue. This will, in turn, significantly impact the way your counterparts react to your statements and questions.

Framing the negotiation is similar to the old saying that the glass can be half full or half empty, depending upon our point of view. It is essential to recognize that if you don't create a specific frame for the negotiation, then you are probably negotiating within the default frame of your counterparts. Framing sets the context and paints a mutual understanding of the discussion.

This relates to the topic of anchoring, which we addressed previously. Framing and anchoring are similar in that they include statements that move your counterpart toward a perspective of the terms being negotiated. You are effectively setting the ground rules for what comes next. They are also similar in that they can be reset multiple times by either party during a negotiation.

Where they differ is that an anchor is typically used to put some specific aspect of the negotiation into a different context (e.g., "Normally, this item sells for $100, but today we are selling it for $24.95."). Framing establishes the agenda and priorities for the entire negotiation (e.g., "Today, we would like to agree about how payroll and benefits will be handled after the merger").

Setting The Frame

If you know that your counterpart is automatically going to focus on the price aspect of a particular transaction, you could frame (or reframe) the negotiation by focusing on the ongoing partnership opportunity associated with the transaction. Often, the best question to ask to derive an appropriate frame for any negotiation is, "Why are we here?" Making use of an agenda is a great way to set and continue to shape the frame. Wherever possible, you should start your negotiations with a clear, results-oriented frame, as this will ensure focus on potential common ground (rather than getting stuck in differences) and bring perspective to the shared interests.

Let's imagine you are considering buying equipment from Paul and you have received and considered his quotation. You could frame the meeting this way: "Thanks again for making time for us today, Paul. We want to explore a little more detail behind your quotation in the hope of reaching an agreement. Do you mind if we address price and delivery timelines as a first step?"

There you have created a strong and positive frame as well as gained agreement on the issues you want to discuss.

A strong frame is a frame where your statement is highly aligned with your desired outcome for discussions. For instance, let's say you are meeting with a client to agree on terms for a new project. An example of a strong framing statement could be: "At the end of this meeting, I would like us to have reached agreement on the start date and duration of the project, as well as pricing levels." When using a strong frame, you bring focus to talks and put your counterparts on notice that you are pursuing their input and perspectives on specific points of interest.

A weak frame is a statement (often an opening statement) that is not really in line with your desired outcome at all. Using the same client meeting as context, an example of a weak framing statement could be: "I just wanted to catch up with you and hear about the latest developments." As you can see, this weak framing statement creates a totally different expectation that is not aligned with your real intent at all (which is to agree on the start date, duration, and pricing levels for the project).

I often see inexperienced negotiators make the mistake of using weak frames because they lack confidence or they are just unclear on what they hope to achieve. Sadly, they are often surprised by the pushback they receive from their counterparts as a result of not having managed their expectations appropriately. A weak frame is not necessarily a bad thing. It depends on the objective of your discussion and can be particularly useful when you have bad news to deliver like an impending increase in price or a change in payment terms.

Gains or Losses

Another way you can use framing to influence negotiations is by deciding on whether you want to frame things in terms of gains or losses. Research into Prospect Theory (Kahneman & Tversky, 1979) has proven that managers weigh potential losses heavier than potential gains, so it is often useful to create momentum toward a decision by using what we call "loss framing" (focusing on what your counterpart stands to lose if they don't accept your offer) rather than only using "gains framing" (focusing on what they stand to gain by accepting your offer). In most sales training programs, there is almost always too much focus on describing the benefits of your solutions, services, and products to counterparts, and not enough focus on describing the risks or losses associated with your counterparts not entering into a relationship with you and your organization. The carrot is nice, but sometimes the fear of the stick gets better results.

Framing Tips

- Framing can shape aspirations. Higher aspirations tend to boost results.

- Highlight concerns about potential losses. Potential losses always loom larger than gains; gains are secondary to not losing.

- Invoke the common ground and emphasize mutual benefits.

- Establish and control the agenda of what will and will not be negotiated.

- Use questioning to frame the situation and call out problems.

- Get your counterpart to identify with your frame by asking, "If you were in my shoes/situation, what would you do?"

- When confronted by a negative frame, provide the other party with alternatives. Move them from decision making to choosing.

Reframing

During the course of deal making, you will likely find situations where it is essential to reframe the conversation, such as when your counterpart has set the frame for the meeting, and it doesn't align with your goals. You may even find that the frame of a conversation goes back and forth several times as counterparts jockey for control. There may also be times where the conversation has drifted away from the stated purpose, and you feel the need to bring it back to the original topic.

Reframing the conversation may be as simple as restating the original topic: "I'd like to get back to the original question of retirement matching for W-2 employees." In some situations, though, it might require a more thorough review of the goals of the meeting: "I agree that it will be important to discuss employee benefits, so let's allocate some time for that this afternoon when we are discussing the silos of operations. Can we take this opportunity now to settle on how ownership will be structured after the merger?"

Framing & Reframing Tools

The frame of a conversation is usually stated in one or two sentences by the person who called the meeting (although there may be strategic reasons for the host to invite the guest to set the frame). Once the frame has been established, the framer may allow the counterpart to respond. The counterpart can either accept the frame or take the opportunity to reframe the meeting.

Example 1

Frame: "I'm calling to discuss the renewal of your contract."

Re-frame: "Thanks for your call. My aim is to understand your needs in more detail to establish whether or not I can offer you a more competitive option."

Example 2

Frame: "I'm calling to discuss the renewal of your contract."

Re-frame: "Thank you for your call; my job is to understand your requirements to determine whether or not we can meet your needs."

Example 3

Frame: "I'm calling to discuss the renewal of your contract. Unfortunately, you are too expensive."

Re-frame: "I understand that price is important to you, let me ask you a few questions to make sure that I understand your situation/ to make sure that we are on the same page."

This last example brings up a vital technique successful negotiators use that I want to address in detail.

Questioning in Negotiation

Questioning is one of the most powerful tools you can use. Unfortunately, it doesn't come naturally to most people. Most of us tend to justify and defend our point of view, position, or interests rather than spending time gathering information from our counterparts, which may result in uncovering additional opportunities for agreement. Mastering questioning can assist you to:

- Reframe the negotiation

- Identify, manage, and overcome objections

- Identify new options and opportunities

- Resolve conflict

- Close a deal

There are some common pitfalls associated with questioning:

- Human nature tends toward being self-focused. People naturally tend to focus on explaining their own positions and interests rather than asking questions about their counterpart's positions and interests.

- People often fail to listen to the their counterparts' answers because they are using the time that their counterpart is talking to prepare their next statement.

- People tend to respond too soon after their counterpart has spoken, and so fail to take the time to gain a full understanding of their counterparts' position and interests and how they relate to their own.

A Model For Asking Questions

Probing and Nurturing Questions

There are probing and nurturing questions that can help you understand precise needs and challenges, which will, in turn, help you to meet those needs with your product/service or solution.

Probing Question: "Why have you decided to implement this system?"

Answer: "Because we've experienced some problems with our existing solution."

Nurturing Question: "Would you please expand on what these problems are and when/how they arose?"

You should prepare at least one or two probing questions covering each negotiation pillar. Make sure that the questions you ask are open ("What can you tell me about your plans for the new building?") and not closed (Yes/No questions like, "Are you planning to use this building for storage?"). This will enable you to identify interests, not just positions.

Be sure to actively listen to the answers provided—not responding immediately, but taking the time to confirm that you understand first—and use nurturing questions to uncover further interests.

You cannot negotiate successfully without questioning. If this is your current style, then you are not likely to move your counterparts toward agreement; you are merely stating, defending, and positioning your needs in the hope that your counterparts will simply exchange their perspectives and desires for yours. It would be much simpler for you to just send them a document summarizing your demands—you certainly don't need to meet with them in person if your only goal is to let your counterparts know what is important to you.

My point here is simply that asking your counterpart questions not only uncovers information you can use, but it can make your counterpart feel valued and more willing to open up to you. It can also help you overcome their objectives, re-prioritize their decision criteria, and move them toward a decision that is favorable to you.

Culturally and personally, some negotiators feel uncomfortable asking questions of their counterpart, but since we are working on the assumption that we all communicate and behave as professionals with expertise and integrity, we should never feel afraid of coming across as demanding or interrogating our counterparties. If that is your concern, learning how to ask questions in a non-aggressive, interested manner will be an important boost to your career for many reasons. The old adage applies: It is often not what you say, but how you say it that is important.

Using The 4 Pillars To Plan Your Questions

When asking questions, another useful framework is the 4 Pillars of Negotiation themselves. That way, you can be sure that you address the negotiation from all the important angles:

- **Why** are you doing this? (Vision)
- **Who** are the players involved in this event? (Relationship)
- **What** are you expecting as a key outcome of this negotiation? (Value)
- **How** will you reach a decision or measure the success of the engagement? (Process)

On the following pages are some simple examples of useful questions to ask:

Vision

Probing Questions

- Why do you have a need for this solution/discussion/meeting?
- What do you expect from this meeting?

Nurturing Questions

- How long have you had this need?
- What will happen if we don't reach an agreement today?
- How will this impact you/ your company?

Value

Probing Questions

- What are the key elements of the deal that you are looking for?
- What research have you done into potential solutions?

Nurturing Questions

- Help me understand how you calculated the values for each element.
- Tell me more about the research method you used.

Relationship

Probing Questions

- Who are the key stakeholders?
- Who will be most impacted by your decisions?

Nurturing Questions

- What would represent success for each stakeholder?
- How are they involved in the decision making process?

Process

Probing Questions

- When would you like to start implementation?
- What timelines for completion do you have in mind?

Nurturing Questions

- Why this particular date?
- What will happen if your team fails to deliver on time?

Questions That Uncover Interests

As we discussed earlier, one of the most important outcomes of negotiation is to uncover and address the unspoken interests behind your counterparts' positions. Doing so allows you to mine for deeper, more meaningful partnership opportunities. Nearly everything your counterpart says has the potential to alert you to a deeper need. Let's look at a handful of statements your counterpart might make that seem innocuous on the surface, but the alert negotiator will see them as opportunities to probe further.

Statement

"Please send me your proposal by the end of the week."

Possible Response Questions

- What do I need to include in the proposal for it to be valuable to you?
- What are your key decision making factors?
- What would help you and your organization to be more efficient and effective right now?"

Statement

"I would like sufficient after-sales support."

Possible Response Questions

What would you consider sufficient after-sales support?

Tell me more about what that looks like to you.

Statement

"I expect better service than I've experienced so far."

Possible Response Questions

- Can you tell me what was unsatisfactory in the past, so I can be clear on how to improve your experience?
- How exactly can I better serve your needs in the future?

Statement

"I think your services/products are too expensive."

Possible Response Questions

- How did you come to that conclusion?
- How do you measure price vs. value?
- Give me an example of a price that seems more appropriate to you.

Statement

"I can't give you the order today."

Possible Response Questions

- What prevents you from giving me the order today?
- What can I do to help you prepare the order?

Handling Objections Through Effective Questioning

To increase your chances of successfully closing a deal, you should anticipate possible objections and practice multiple ways of responding to them. This is a critical part of preparing for a negotiation that many people miss. As a result, they are caught off-guard by objections and react with ill-prepared statements of fact instead of responding thoughtfully.

First, acknowledge the statement. After all, your counterpart is entitled to her opinions, even if you disagree with her. It is worth noting that you provoke most of the objections you receive. While it might be tempting to believe that your counterpart is a knucklehead who doesn't recognize the value of your offer, the truth is that something you said caused them to push back. You may have led with your evidence and your counterpart is simply noting their objections to your evidence. Accepting this truth requires humility most people do not possess, but this is a level of personal development that facilitates unbelievable deal-making results.

Second, ask questions to identify where the disconnect lies. Remember, the only reality in this meeting is your counterpart's perception of reality. It doesn't matter what you say; it only matters what your counterpart hears. No matter how artfully you may have made your case, if they don't share your view of what you said, you need to know why and adjust accordingly. Asking questions not only gets you the information you are seeking, but it also honors your counterpart and demonstrates that you value them. It may also provide you with important strategic information about your counterpart's values, perspective, beliefs, and fears that you can use to shape your message later.

Consider these common objections and think about how you might use questions to respond to each. Again, make sure that you acknowledge the objection and ask questions to gain a better understanding of what is behind this objection:

Objection

"Your price is too high. You must reduce your price."

Possible Responses

- "I would like to understand your needs in more detail to establish whether or not I can offer you a more competitive option. I understand that price is important to you, let me ask you a few questions to make sure that I understand your situation/make sure that we are on the same page."

- "How do you measure price versus value?"

- "If I can find a way to deal with the price issue that satisfies you, would you buy today?"

- "Suppose we could find a way to get around the pricing issue. Would there be any reason against going ahead with this purchase?"

- "Apart from price, what is that you like about our value offering?"

- "What are your goals for the next twelve months?"

- "Is the price reduction the only issue, or are there any other challenges that you are currently facing?"

- "Obviously you must have a reason for saying that. Would you mind if I asked what it is?"

- "Under what circumstances would you be prepared to pay this price?"

- "Just out of curiosity, what presents you with higher risk at the moment, paying a little bit more than you expected or losing the profits we have spoken about?"

- "What do you take as a measure of cost effectiveness?"

Price negotiation is a necessary step in any commercial transaction. As a seller, if you understand the buyer's motivation, you will be better positioned to deal with price objections and engage in price negotiation. The better you understand your customers' interests and motivations, the better you can shift the focus from price to the benefits of your offer and ultimately protect your margins.

Objection

"I need more time to make a decision."

Possible Responses

- "What exactly are you still uncertain about?"

- "What concerns do you have regarding this purchase?"

- "What do I need to put in the proposal for it to be valuable?"

- "What are your decision criteria?"

- "I understand that you want more time to think. What are your thoughts about the reasons for and the reasons against buying now?"

Objection

"I want to shop around."

Possible Responses

- "Absolutely, everyone likes to explore the market before making the final decision. What would make you choose one product over the other?"

- "What questions do you have that I could answer right now?"

- "What are your decision making factors?"

- "Just out of curiosity, who else will you be talking to?"

Objection

"We are happy with what we have at the moment."

Possible Responses

- "Under what circumstances would you consider an alternative provider of XYZ?"

- "What criteria do we have to meet to start a business relationship with you?"

Crucial Caveat About Questioning

With all this discussion about asking good questions, it would be understandable if you took the view one negotiation research project advocated: the more questions you ask the more successful your negotiations will be. While it's always tempting to postulate an easy, linear correlation like this, it is not based on reality. Questions draw out (mostly) useful information and do your counterpart the honor of ascribing value to their thoughts and feelings, but you can ask questions all day and still not reach an agreement. There is no linear correlation between questions and success. It is only one of the clubs in your bag. It is a powerful club, but it is not a guarantee of success.

Key Takeaways from Chapter Eight

- Framing the conversation with an opening statement that manages expectations is a powerful way to ensure that all parties are on the same page and ready to engage in a smooth conversation.

- The party that called for the meeting usually sets the frame and expectations for the meeting, although there may be times when it is suitable to defer to the other party.

- It is possible, and sometimes desirable, to re-frame a conversation if the original frame does not suit your needs or if the conversation drifts away from the original objectives.

- Asking questions of your counterpart not only honors them and validates their perspective, but it also allows you to uncover their interests, respond to objections, and clarify their position.

- Asking questions has many benefits, but it does not guarantee an agreement.

"One who never asks either knows everything or nothing."

— Malcom Forbes

Apply It To Your Situation

1. Identify three things you learned from this chapter that you want to begin implementing in your negotiations. Highlight the one you want to do first.

   _____

   _____

   _____

2. Describe how you have used framing in the past, even if you were doing it unknowingly.

   _____

   _____

   _____

   _____

3. What has been your use of questions in the past? How could this new understanding of questioning help you to be more effective with your questioning?

   _____

   _____

   _____

   _____

4. How have you handled or prevented objections in the past? What have your results been? How could this questioning model be more effective?

   _____

   _____

   _____

   _____

5. What did you learn about negotiation in this chapter that surprised or enlightened you?

   _____

   _____

   _____

   _____

Chapter Nine: Team Negotiation and Structure

Executive Summary

- Your success as a negotiator is directly tied to your thorough preparation and planning.

- A team-based approach to negotiation allows people to fill roles that best suit their strengths.

- A small team with one member focused on the relationship, one focused on tasks and data, and another to observe the nonverbal interactions is often more effective than a large team.

- When individuals are not clear on their roles in a negotiation, it makes them feel uncomfortable and may lead them to act out in ways that weaken your position.

- Many people—including professional negotiators—fall into the trap of neglecting the logistics of a meeting, including securing the meeting site, preparing an agenda, and communicating consistently prior to the meeting.

A Note To Those Who Are Still "Winging It"

At this point in my live training workshops, I can usually identify two groups of participants: those who are taking the material seriously and are going to adjust their behavior and can expect to see a significant improvement in their results, and those who won't. I suspect those two audiences exist among those who read this book, as well.

I am going to make a bold statement here, and I hope you will indulge me for one more paragraph. Although it may seem pedestrian compared to the previous material we've covered, your determination to consistently apply the techniques in the next three chapters will have as much impact on your negotiation success as the other topics we have covered.

There are aspects of the process, preparation, and logistics that, while they might seem secondary to strategy, tactics, and objectives, have every bit as much influence on your results. You can get everything else right and still fail to achieve your negotiation goals every single time if you neglect these issues.

If you have invested the effort to read this far, I salute you for your diligence. If you still plan to go on from here just "winging it" regarding your negotiation preparation, then nothing I have said in this book will profit you much, no matter how well you apply it.

You may be tempted to breeze through these chapters. Please don't. These considerations will sharpen and fine tune your negotiations on every level, position you as a true professional in the minds of your counterparts, and give you a competitive advantage in every interaction. Failure to apply them will have exactly the opposite effects.

Join The Team

While many of your day-to-day negotiations will occur between you and one other person, there will be times when you need to organize a team to conduct a specific negotiation. Team negotiations can be challenging to manage, especially if the team members are not clear on their respective roles and responsibilities.

Human beings attach significant value to the roles they fill. If you neglect to assign clear roles and responsibilities to each member of the team, they will likely feel a sense of insecurity because their presence on the team is not justified.

Team members who are unclear or insecure in their role will be tempted to speak out of turn, looking for an opportunity to participate and justify their presence. After all, who just wants to sit quietly and watch the negotiation take place without them? To prevent that uncertainty and insecurity from vesting in your team and creating opportunities for arbitrage for your counterparts, be sure to have a clear division of roles and responsibilities across all the members of the team. If someone does not have a clearly identifiable role, leave them out.

Play To People's Strengths

As much as possible, make sure these assignments align well with each individual's strengths. Some people are excellent with managing facts and figures, while others chafe at the first sign of a spreadsheet; know which is which before assigning anyone to conduct research. By the same token, don't ask the natural "accommodator" to play hardball with your counterpart.

Almost all team-based negotiations involve at least two distinct types of roles: relationship-focused roles and task-focused roles. It is essential to ensure that each team member is assigned a role that suits them to prevent arbitrage and misalignment.

Most negotiations go through three distinct phases—the first is focused on the relationship, the second moves into the content to be discussed, and the third goes back to the relationship elements. It is often difficult for one person to play both the task-focused role and the relationship-focused role. One usually has to be focused on the details of the deal at hand while the other is managing and cultivating the relationship. It can confuse your counterpart (and even you) if one person is playing both these roles, so it is often easier to have different individuals on your team, representing each role.

Additional Players

There may also be situations where you need the support of legal counsel, technical specialists, or other resources in the negotiation. In many cases, they will fill a secondary role on the team, so you should introduce them as supporting resources with specific duties, lest your counterpart is tempted to engage with them separately at will. Managing expectations and access will be critical. If lines of communication become unclear, you may inadvertently abdicate your role on the team to someone who doesn't share your interests, preferences, or working knowledge of your counterpart.

It is sometimes useful to have an observer present on your team—this is a person who has no role other than observing what is taking place and perhaps calling for adjournments from time to time. Because this person is not involved in the negotiation, he or she can focus on understanding the context and consistency of the communication that takes place on both sides of the talks, along with specifically studying the body language of your counterparts. You will be astonished at the valuable information picked up by a neutral observer. The moment an observer starts getting involved in formulating arguments or responding to counterparts, then they are no longer an observer and will not be able to focus on the nonverbal communication and contextual elements as before.

Interaction Among Teams—A Common Misconception

Often, when the topic of team negotiation comes up in one of my live courses, someone will ask if it is better to look at the person who is speaking at any given moment or to look at your counterparts. Many sales training programs teach young salespeople to observe the sales professional they are shadowing during sales calls. That is all well and good; the new salesperson can learn much from watching their trainer's mannerisms and posture.

In a negotiation setting, on the other hand, it might seem courteous to look at your team member when they are speaking, but in doing so, you miss out on your counterparts' non-verbal reaction to what is being said. They may be exhibiting excitement, boredom, anger, disinterest, surprise, or a host of other emotions. This is useful information that can guide the rest of the decisions you make during and after the negotiation. Don't miss out on that data.

By the same token, your counterparts may be showing you their cards through their body language when one of their own team members is speaking. That can also be useful information. We'll come back to body language in a later chapter, but it merits mention as we discuss team dynamics.

A Word About Taking Notes

Some people like to take notes during a negotiation, but in my opinion, you're much better off writing down a few notes at the end of the meeting, so you don't miss any of the non-verbal data in the room. Imagine some of the negotiation greats like Nelson Mandela or Abraham Lincoln interrupting a negotiation to say, "I'm sorry, let me just write that down." If anything, they would have somebody else taking notes for them to review later, but they wouldn't take their eyes off their counterpart, looking for any kind of signal to better understand what is being said.

So, if it's your habit to write down notes, stop. You will learn much more by not writing down a single thing. I know this flies in the face of all of the academic world and most of the business world, but taking notes in a negotiation is not going to aid your understanding; it will much more likely cause you to miss some critical data. If you absolutely must make a note, keep it to a single word or bullet point.

One Final Thought About Teams

The bigger your team, the longer the negotiation will take, as each team member will usually want to contribute and may end up adding levels of complexity to an otherwise simple matter. While it may be wise to surround yourself with a large group of expert advisors from several disciplines, to reach agreement quickly, it is usually preferable to have a small team of negotiators.

Here's what we know from the research that we've done: usually, when you see a large team come into a negotiation, it is a safe assumption that they aren't optimally prepared to negotiate. When you have a lot of people, you have to manage the roles and expectations. That redirects your energy and attention away from your counterpart and your objectives.

I've seen this happen as well: a negotiator hears that his counterpart is bringing a team of five or six, while he was only planning to bring two people with him. So, in an act of desperation, he conscripts the help of some extra co-workers. They sit in the meeting without any preparation and no understanding of their role, and after about half an hour, one of them decides she needs to say something to justify her presence in the meeting. Because she hasn't been adequately prepared and assigned a legitimate role on the team, she blurts out something the lead negotiator was saving for later. It's not her fault; had she been prepared with a proper agenda and told the strategic order of how the cards will be played, she would have known to wait.

It would have been better to come into the negotiation with a smaller team with clear roles and responsibilities.

I don't wish to suggest that there is a hard and fast rule for team size (remember our golf analogy); each negotiation will dictate its own parameters. As a general rule of thumb, a smaller team is better because there is so much less for you to manage. But more often than not, you will want to have a relationship-focused person on your team, as well as a task-focused person, and possibly an observer. All other contributors should belong to your secondary/support team unless the needs of the negotiation dictate otherwise.

Structure

As American statesman Benjamin Franklin (and countless others) quipped, "By failing to prepare, you are preparing to fail." Structure before, during, and after your meetings is critical. It not only helps you to focus on your objectives but will help you to display confidence and professionalism. You can tell when someone is enjoying the confidence of thorough preparation, and when they are missing it. When you have observed it in others, hasn't it caused you to take them more seriously?

Structure includes several elements, including:

Pre-negotiation Communications

It is often a good idea to send an email or invitation to your counterparts ahead of the negotiation. This might be a simple calendar invitation to confirm the time and venue, but it can also be a handy way to introduce the participants, review the topics to be discussed, and exchange detailed documents.

A quick email can not only be a convenient way to save time during the meeting; it can also be a powerful way to frame the negotiation in your favor before you even arrive. Of course, all parties must manage appropriate confidentiality.

The Agenda

Speaking of framing, one of the critical documents in any negotiation is an agenda. An agenda is an excellent way to gain agreement on the topics and issues you will discuss. To demonstrate your commitment to your counterpart's interests, you could use a pre-meeting email to list the agenda items of both parties for their consideration.

After they have read through the list and suggested changes, you could send a final combined agenda for the meeting. This gives the impression of solidarity and working on the same team, as opposed to haggling over whose agenda items will get preference.

Meeting Minutes

It is crucial that you maintain some form of a written record of issues discussed during your negotiations, particularly if your discussions span weeks or months. You should appoint someone to make a note of the crucial items. At the end of the meeting, take a moment to verbally summarize what has been discussed, then follow up the same day, if possible, with a letter or email that confirms what was discussed for permanent record. If there is any dispute over what was said, it can be brought up in either of these two formats. This prevents episodes of "he said/she said" at your next meeting.

Meeting Venue

It is astounding how many times people neglect to check on the details of the meeting venue, including facilities, equipment, schedules, staffing, and so on. This is an essential aspect of being ready for a meeting, particularly if you have chosen a neutral location like a hotel conference room. Many negotiations have been stalled, delayed, or shut down altogether because someone failed to confirm the room reservation, booked the wrong date, or forgot to order a whiteboard or tables.

These may seem like minor details, but if you've ever had a negotiation derailed because your office forgot to pay the deposit on the meeting room, you understand that details can make or break you.

On the other hand, I am aware of at least one case where a company won a major contract that would otherwise have been out of their league in part because they had the foresight to order specific flowers and hors d'oeuvres for the meeting room that they knew their counterpart liked. That attention to detail that others had overlooked helped them win over a big client.

I will come back to this matter of the venue in a later chapter because there are some practical ways you can use the venue to your advantage.

Key Takeaways from Chapter Nine

- Adequate preparation before a negotiation not only gives you confidence going in, it positions you as a professional in your counterparts' minds, which can provide a significant strategic advantage.

- Failing to prepare and overlooking seemingly insignificant details can derail a negotiation before it starts.

- Clear, concise, and accurate communication before, during, and after a negotiation can prevent embarrassing mistakes, allows you to frame the meeting and agenda to your advantage, and can also create an environment where your counterpart feels valued, respected, and unified.

- Assembling a team for negotiations can allow you to assign roles in the meeting that play to people's strengths, like relationship-builder, task-manager, and observer.

- Having too many people on your team or poorly-defined assignments can cause people to feel insecure in their roles and speak out of turn in an effort to justify their presence. It is better to have fewer people with clearly defined roles than a large team.

- Sometimes, it is advisable to have legal counsel or technical specialists on your team, but be sure their roles are clear to both parties or your counterpart may address them outside the scope of their role.

"In planning for battle I have always found that plans are useless, but planning is indispensable."

—General Dwight D Eisenhower.

Apply It To Your Situation

1. Identify three things you learned from this chapter that you want to begin implementing in your daily life. Highlight the one you want to do first.

    _____

    _____

    _____

    _____

2. Describe how a team approach, with clearly-defined roles for each member, can enhance your negotiations?

    _____

    _____

    _____

    _____

3. Describe an area of your life where you would like to be more effective in your preparation. How would it improve things?

    _____

    _____

    _____

    _____

4. What did you learn about negotiation in this chapter that surprised or enlightened you?

    _____

    _____

    _____

    _____

Chapter Ten: Managing The Climate

Executive Summary

- The fourth of the 4 Pillars of Negotiation is Relationship. Mastering the "soft skills" of human interaction is crucial for negotiation success.

- The "soft skills" that make business work—rapport, kindness, honor, personal grooming, and others—have fallen out of style in many cultures, giving those who still possess them a significant advantage.

- Humans are not machines; they make decisions based on emotions, perceptions, and inputs from their environment that are not purely logical.

- Honor is a master key to success in business. You extend honor to your counterpart by how you conduct yourself during your negotiation and how you engage with them.

- Since research shows that 93% of all communication is nonverbal, mastery of body language—being aware of your own nonverbal messaging and learning to properly read your counterpart's—is vital to correctly navigating a negotiation.

- Preparing the meeting space to foster an environment that supports your strategy and objectives is a best practice for negotiation success.

- When dealing with counterparts from other countries, ethnicities, religions—or even other companies—you must recognize and honor the nuances of the cultures they represent if you are to be successful. A small cultural faux pas can derail a good negotiation.

- There are at least six core principles of persuasion that master negotiators use to move their counterparts toward a favorable outcome.

We're Not Dealing With Machines

If this were a book about programming machines to negotiate, we could talk about entering data in a way that would assure the desired output, and that would be the end of it.

Negotiating with humans is not linear or straightforward, and our strategies, tactics, and techniques need to reflect the inherent complexities of dealing with humans.

We have already shown how people are not purely logical like machines; we make decisions led as much by our emotions as by our intellect (some observers say that we tend to give higher priority to our emotional cores over our logical cores). As we prepare to engage with our human counterparts, we must be ready to address their emotional drivers, as well as their rational drivers.

Just like you can't successfully play golf by swinging the same club the exact same way in all circumstances, you can't walk into every negotiation and use the same scripts and expect to be successful. Every human is unique from all others, and the same person can have completely opposite reactions to the same stimulus from one moment to the next, all other things being equal. This is part of what makes us human.

The Fourth Pillar

We are moving now to the last of our 4 Pillars of Negotiation: Relationship. Throughout the preceding chapters, we have talked about selecting and developing a strategy for each negotiation, choosing appropriate tactics for engaging our counterparts, identifying our objectives (and theirs), framing the discussion, setting anchors, and making concessions. All of these activities are measurable ways to move the negotiation forward, and nearly all of them involve words.

According to research by professor of psychology Albert Mehrabian in the 1970s, as much as ninety-three percent of all communication is non-verbal. The words we exchange with our counterparts represent only a tiny fraction of the messages being communicated.

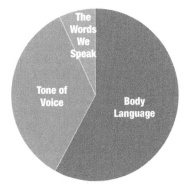

That is why, whether we are setting the terms of a multi-national business deal or settling an argument with a family member, we need to be at least as interested in the intangible, non-verbal aspects of our interactions as we are in the words we choose.

In this final pillar, we are going to be dealing less with things you can quantify (e.g., numbers, strategies, etc.) and more with what is sometimes called "soft skills," like how to create a specific atmosphere in the negotiation room, how to greet your counterparts when they arrive, and how to position individuals around the room for maximum effect.

My wife, Linda, is an expert's expert when it comes to interpersonal skills, dress, grooming, and posture. She has even written a book and created a website (www. lindpaige.com) on building your personal style brand. I will be referring to her often in this section. From time to time, when her schedule allows, she gives an unbelievably high-impact presentation on communication styles during my two-day open access negotiation workshops. I may be biased, but I believe everyone should attend her training in this area at least once.

We'll start with some of the most basic aspects of this pillar and move to more advanced considerations.

As we do, make sure whatever approach you take communicates precisely the message you intend. Also, remember that the way your counterpart perceives your action is their reality, not necessarily what you intended. Your intentions have no bearing on what they perceive. To some, certain behaviors communicate that you are weak and unsure of yourself, while others might understand the same behavior as a sign of strength. The better your pre-negotiation research on your counterpart, the more accurately you will adopt your communications to their viewpoint.

Courtesy

This might seem like a rudimentary topic for professional adults to mention in a business book, but while courtesy is one of those matters that is easy to overlook, we do so at our own peril. It is never acceptable to be impolite or rude when we negotiate.

Surprisingly, the skills of decorum have taken a back seat in the modern workplace. You may have observed this yourself. Whether it is a reflection of our culture's gradual decline toward self-absorption and entitlement, or just a lack of training in interpersonal skills, it is all the more glaring in the negotiation environment. The Rule of Reciprocity will destroy you if you lack courtesy.

You do not need to like people to treat them kindly. Their beliefs, habits, and behaviors can be diametrically opposed to your objectives, your values—even your very existence—and you can still be courteous to them.

One of the best examples I can offer is South Africa's revolutionary political leader, Nelson Mandela. He was one of the toughest negotiators in recent memory, yet he was respected for his uncanny ability to treat his counterparts with dignity, even those who had treated him with contempt and unfiltered hatred. He even interacted courteously with the AWB (a South African resistance movement similar to the Ku Kux Klan of the United States). He asserted that he disagreed with their views but held up their right to hold and even express those views. This way, Mandela made himself amenable to his enemies, even as he was putting them in their place, so to speak. Consider what he managed to achieve in his political career.

To be tough doesn't require you to be rude or nasty. In fact, a competitive stance can be enhanced by keeping a sincere smile on your face. You can be firm and polite at the same time. This way, you allow your counterparts to "save face," and they remain engaged in the negotiation process.

Greetings

The first few seconds of any meeting transmit volumes of information into the subconscious minds of everyone involved. How that information is received and understood is as individual as the participants. Set the tone you intend with a well-planned greeting.

Your greeting sets the tone for your interaction, usually within seconds of the first eye contact. What you say (and what you don't say) communicates more than your words could ever hold. Do you make eye contact with your counterpart? Do you call them by their name or ask their name if you do not know it? Do you extend a handshake (or bow, as the culture may dictate)? Do you smile as you greet them?

You can communicate acceptance and friendship or contempt with your greeting—consciously or unconsciously. The more you know about your counterparts' preferences (and their perception of you), the better equipped you will be to use the appropriate greetings.

Communication Style

There are countless books, videos, and courses on the market regarding interpersonal communication, but they tend to overlook one important factor: people are different, and their communication styles vary by personality. Most of us in the professional world have been conditioned to believe that there is one style of communication for business or professional environments, and nothing else is acceptable. I think we shortchange ourselves when we embrace that thinking.

As we explored in the NBI™ personality model, some people are more task-focused, while others are more relationship-focused. Neither is right or wrong, but they are different, and they manifest in ways that may be abrasive to each other. If you are jovial and effervescent, you might have a hard time negotiating with someone who is more staid and unemotional, and they might have a hard time with you. Your first instinct would be to avoid someone like that, but that would be a mistake.

Human nature is to gravitate toward people we perceive to be like us and chafe at those who are different. Unless you buck that tendency, you will literally leave a fortune on the table. The more effectively you interact with people different from you, the more successful (and wealthy) you will be. Just as some of the most significant breakthroughs in business have come from unexpected combinations of businesses and industries (think of how FedEx combined air freight and parcel delivery), getting beyond your personality preferences will open up "out-of-the-box" opportunities that could be worth billions of dollars. Your breakthrough business might literally be on the other side of a person whose communication style irritates you.

Certainly, personality styles are not to be used as an excuse for unprofessional, rude, or unmannerly behavior, but if we squelch personal expression in the name of "professionalism," we risk driving away creativity, empathy, enthusiasm, warmth, and other valuable human attributes that don't always fit in dark suits.

Rapport

Some sales professionals are trained in "mirroring." If I get into a conversation with someone who is talking fast and gesturing with their hands, I will speed up my pace and move my hands more.

That's not normal for me. Why would I do it?

I do it to make the other person feel honored and valued. If they think I am like them, they are more likely to feel comfortable with me. Am I being fake? No, I don't do it in an unnatural way—that would be mimicking, which is dishonoring to the other person. I am merely taking a step in their direction to make them feel at home. Sincerity is always recognized and appreciated. It can be as simple as toning down your volume and pace to match another's, to create harmony.

In the context of negotiation, it is good to be "in sync" with your counterpart when you are in agreement. Equally, it is essential to break the rapport when you are not in agreement. Failing to do this might lead to misunderstandings, as your counterpart might think you are in agreement when you are not. Rapport is built by lending yourself to the relationship, so be sure to use any opportunity to build trust and visibility, but be sure your nonverbal signals are clear.

Vocabulary

There are people in this world who have cultivated expansive vocabularies and like to use them to talk over people. It gives the speaker an unmerited sense of importance. In reality, it communicates arrogance, which is never conducive to building rapport that will advance your objectives (unless your objective is to make people dislike you). If you are speaking to a room full of doctors, your vocabulary should reflect that, but you should always adjust your vocabulary to the level of the room.

Voice

I am physically larger than most of the people around me and I have a loud voice, so it is easy for people to perceive me as being aggressive and intimidating, even if I don't mean to be. At one point in my life, I liked to use that to my advantage. I am not proud of that.

It became a stumbling block in the growth of my marriage. I am quite a bit larger than my wife and have a much louder voice, and had cultivated a pattern of using my size as leverage. To be successful at home and at work, I had to relearn the skill of speaking to others. I am very fortunate that Linda is a strong, confident, assertive woman, and I am grateful that she was not about to let me push her around. To be a successful negotiator—indeed, a successful human being—it behooves me to be mindful of how loudly or quietly I speak, and Linda holds me accountable in that arena.

On the other side of the coin, mumbling and whispering are usually perceived as signs of weakness in the same manner as a slouching body posture, so I don't advocate that, either. As with most things, there is a sweet spot somewhere in the middle. Now, if you've raised children, you probably have come to realize that there are times when lowering your voice to just above a whisper and clearly enunciating your words can help to make your point abundantly clear. It works for employees and negotiation counterparts in much the same way.

Research also shows that humans prefer the tone of a low-pitched voice to a shrill, high-pitched voice. You seldom hear broadcasters with high-pitched, nasal voices. If you have a high or immature-sounding voice, consider vocal coaching. It would be unfortunate to be brilliant and not be taken seriously because of something as trivial as the tone of your voice. However, because it is a subconscious tendency, the prudent approach is to take appropriate steps to eliminate anything that would distract your counterpart's attention away from the content of your message, just as you would not enter a meeting with a crumpled shirt and stained tie.

This is all good self-awareness and preparation.

Personal Appearance

Clothing styles come and go. Neckties go in and out of fashion in the business world. Certain personalities will tend to chafe against having to wear pressed shirts and slacks. Cities with warm climates or large recreational industries, like Orlando, Florida have drifted away from the traditional corporate dress.

None of this excuses a sloppy personal appearance.

As my wife, Linda, says, presentation is important. You are an Ambassador, a walking billboard of how you view yourself, how you approach your work, and what you think about the people around you. Unfair as it may seem, people judge your competence by your outward appearance. You do it to others, too. You know you do. Go walk the aisles at Walmart or any mall for that matter and tell me what you observe about people based on nothing other than their outward appearance.

Wrinkled clothing communicates that you do not pay attention to detail. Wearing ripped, worn, or threadbare jeans to work shows people that you don't esteem your co-workers. Showing up to a professional setting in a t-shirt and sandals communicates contempt to the workplace and the people in it.

The media likes to portray highly successful people like Mark Zuckerberg at work in a t-shirt and sneakers with a hoodie. They make us think it communicates that we are in charge of our own destiny or we are "sticking it to the man," but it does no such thing in the real world. It communicates immaturity, selfishness, and a smug attitude. You might remember when Mr. Zuckerberg appeared to give testimony before the United States House of Representatives: he wore a suit and tie every day he was there. Why? His appearance communicated esteem to the people and the environment, whether or not he harbored it in his heart.

Personal hygiene used to be taught in schools, as well as at home. Those days are largely gone, except in good families. Do you bathe regularly? Manicure your hair, skin, and nails? Wash and iron your clothes? My wife, Linda, charges men and women alike to get up, dress up, and put their best foot forward. Good grooming communicates confidence, and confidence in negotiation is absolutely essential.

You are welcome to be casual when you want to be casual, but your appearance communicates esteem or contempt to the people around you. If you want people to believe that you care nothing about their opinion or about honoring them with your appearance, you will limit your ability to negotiate effectively—especially in a business or professional setting.

What would you wear if you were invited to have an audience with a world leader? Would you not put on your best attire? I know that in some circles it has become fashionable to show contempt for heads of state, but that reflects more on the character of the people who do it than the officials. Until recently, it would have been considered deeply odious to wear a t-shirt and jeans to have an audience with the President of the United States, the Queen of England, or some other dignitary. Contemptible. I hope our world returns quickly to the high level of honor we used to show to leaders (and to each other), no matter your political persuasion. Why would you not treat the people across the negotiation table from you with the same honor and respect in the way you dress?

If you want to be taken seriously, you need to take yourself seriously. Personal style—what you wear—has everything to do with what you are saying.

How do you want people to see you? What is your personal brand? The successful negotiator knows exactly what kind of message he or she wants to convey.

Maybe it's not fair that men ogle women in tight, short skirts and cleavage-baring tops. That is not an aspect of human nature we are equipped to change. On the other hand, if you are a woman and this is your manner in a business setting, Linda and I would challenge you to ask yourself: why am I wearing revealing clothing?

Some women like to wear skin-tight clothing because it distracts their male colleagues and makes their female colleagues feel insecure. That's a leverage tactic and it can be as destructive as it is effective. Use it at your own risk. I won't judge you for it, but I won't pretend that it won't cause you problems. It is a risky game to place and it usually compromises your credibility.

It is good practice to treat everyone with honor in your personal appearance, especially in a negotiation setting. You can use your clothing and hygiene to raise the bar of professionalism in the room. You can also use it to show contempt or to be distracting. What you wear will initiate reciprocity in the same way as what you say.

Personal Space

All cultures have different levels of comfort with regards to their use of space, as do individuals within each culture. Each of us has a unique spatial comfort zone on three levels:

Intimate Zone: Zero to 18 inches. This is the most important spatial zone, across cultures. This space is reserved for loving and fighting. Within this zone, we feel comfortable with our spouse (or lover), children, doctors, and hairdressers. Invading another person's intimate zone can be threatening and might result in that individual taking a defensive stance.

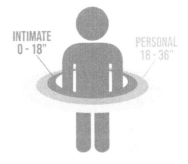

Personal Zone: 18 to 36 inches. This is usually a comfortable zone for approaching people at parties, social functions, and friendly gatherings. This is a comfortable distance to shake hands and exchange business cards.

Social Zone: 36 to 72 inches. We stand at this distance from strangers or people we don't know very well.

When people feel that they don't have enough personal space, they become distracted from the contents of the conversation. They might scan the area for a path of escape and avoid direct eye contact. Every human has their own comfortable space, so it is important to recognize and respond to the other person's nonverbal cues.

The old rule of thumb suggests that, "When in Rome, do as the Romans do," but best practice is to put your counterparts' comfort above your own. If your Asian counterpart comes to your office in the United States, they might be prepared to do business as Westerners do. However, you would do well to make offers in line with their local customs, such as the lunch menu or the pace of your talks. You can only gain from making this investment. As solid relationships are cemented, these gestures will smooth out difficult discussion points later. Honor is not restricted to a location.

Body Gestures and Posture

Experienced negotiators will not just be listening to what people are saying during a negotiation; they will also closely observe nonverbal communication, including posture, gestures, and facial expressions.

Body language is a crucial component of communication, and the nonverbal messages you communicate can either hamper or support what you are saying. Here are a few of the messages we communicate without words, whether we mean to or not:

Eye Contact

Good eye contact builds and maintains rapport, but you should not give attention to just one or two people when there are others in the room, or you might make the others feel uncomfortable. Eye contact is particularly important when discussing money. Trust and confidence must be firmly grounded when discussing price.

Hand Gestures

Some people are highly demonstrative with their hands when they speak, and don't mean anything by it. However, some hand gestures can be seen as aggressive and controlling by different people. If you see your counterparts' facial expression and posture becoming defensive, you might need to limit your hand gestures.

Handshakes

This is a crucial part of the greeting, and you need to understand how to introduce yourself professionally and comfortably at this stage of the relationship. There is a vast range of social norms across borders and cultures, and it is not sufficient to read a book about cultural nuances on the plane en route to your meeting. The handshake/ hand greeting says a lot about people, and wise people will know how to identify (and counter) power plays from domineering counterparts before the negotiation takes place. The male/female dynamic of physical interaction can also enhance or dampen people's opinions of you from the outset. I encourage you to develop a keen sense of awareness on this topic.

Hand/Mouth Movements

You will be signaling strong messages if your hand/mouth gestures are frequent and noticeable. The "hand-over-mouth" gesture is often associated with mistrust, as covering our mouths (particularly during pricing discussions) is indicative of subconsciously hiding what we are saying.

The Nervous System

You need to be aware of how your body responds under pressure, whether it is during a presentation or across the boardroom table in your negotiations. Sweating, hives, trembling, fidgeting, playing with your hair, and other unconscious behaviors communicate insecurity. Understanding your body and how it reacts to pressure is an essential element of self-awareness in communication.

Gender Interactions

Many individuals find it challenging to identify what is and is not acceptable regarding male/female physical interactions. Apart from cross-cultural preferences, many people have trouble behaving normally and in a relaxed fashion in a monocultural social environment. This can lead to embarrassment, awkwardness, and even a loss of respect. Ask a woman how the "wet-lettuce" or "dead fish" male handshake, affects her respect and interest toward that man. Similarly, while men like to compete with and achieve alongside their male counterparts in the business world, don't mistake chivalry for discrimination. Heaven forbid we refuse gentlemanly gestures in the boardroom merely to maintain our view of gender equality.

There is a massive social upheaval taking place around gender, and numerous books have been written (and are being written) about this one topic. Just when you think you know what the new rules are, you meet someone who finds them offensive. A spectrum of gender norms and philosophies is developing in both the Western and Eastern worlds. This is a hot-button topic that is melting down whole industries as we speak. Be aware of legal considerations and your company's preferences regarding gender issues.

Rules for Reading Body Language

Globally-renowned expert on the subject of body language, Allan Pease, shares some important nuances that are important for us to understand. The danger in making assumptions regarding body language is that a misunderstanding of the signals could influence the course of your discussion and adversely impact your negotiation. Be sure to gain an understanding of how body language works, across cultures and genders, and this will enhance your abilities as a negotiator.

Rule #1: Always read body language in clusters rather than isolated movements and postures. Like any spoken language, body language is composed of both words and sentences.

Each gesture is like a single word, and one word might have several different meanings. Gestures come in sentences. A body language sentence, just like a verbal sentence, needs at least three words to be accurately interpreted. Always look at gesture clusters for correct reading.

For example, if I have my arms crossed, it might mean that I'm bored, that I'm closed to your ideas, or it might just say that I'm comfortable. However, crossed arms combined with looking around and avoiding eye contact will convey a different message. If your counterpart is sitting cross-legged and arms folded, it would be natural to assume she is disinterested and closed to the conversation, but that might not be the case. She might be uncomfortable in her chair or suffering back pain. Take a moment to ask a question to understand the signals.

Rule #2: Look for congruence. Research shows that nonverbal signs carry about five times as much impact as the verbal channel, and when the two don't match or are incongruent, people (especially women) rely on the nonverbal message and disregard the verbal content.

This means you should use your body language to support your verbal communication, specifically when you wish to emphasize something. When you're trying to interpret body language, look specifically to see if the body language supports and is in line with their verbal communication.

For example, if your counterpart tells you that he's interested in what you have to say, but then glances at his watch and reads is notes while you are talking, then it is probably safe to assume that he is not really interested in what you have to say.

Rule #3: All body language gestures should be considered in the context in which they occur. For example, being fidgety will have an entirely different meaning in an interview for a new job than it would if you were sitting in cold, wet weather waiting for a train or bus.

Body Language Key Points

While this is by no means a comprehensive list of nonverbal cues, and you need to view them through the filters of clusters, congruence, and context, the more you recognize your own behaviors, the better able you will be to build a vocabulary of gestures that communicate specific messages to your counterpart. You will also have an easier time recognizing the cues you are receiving.

Defensiveness/Suspicion/Doubtfulness

- Not looking at you
- Arms crossed
- Feet/body pointing toward an exit
- Touching/rubbing nose
- Hand over mouth
- Frowning

Non-reassuring, Bored, or Evaluating Signs

- Scribbling
- Drumming on table
- Hand-to-face gestures
- Chewing earpiece of glasses
- Stroking chin

Positive Nonverbal Signs

- Nodding approval
- Vocal sounds of approval
- Leaning forward
- Smiling
- Open arms, palms up

Body Language Don'ts

- Hair-twirling—incompetence, and uncertainty
- Placing your hand in front of your mouth—anxiety about your competence, lying
- Rubbing your arm/leg—anxiety about your competence, uncertainty
- Slumped posture—boredom, alienation

Defensive Body Language

- Leaning back or away
- Positioning body to exclude partner, pointing feet or entire body toward an exit
- Turning face away from partner
- Shaking head horizontally (negatively)
- Assuming an incongruent (dissimilar) body posture
- Making excessive postural shifts, fidgeting, tapping, or jiggling a foot, maintaining a fixed or rigid body posture
- Elevating one's self—standing tall
- Holding head and-or body erect, tilting head back
- Increasing distance between self and partner or invading partner's personal space
- Maintaining a closed body posture (crossing or locking arms/legs or camouflaging body crosses)
- Engaging in highly expansive gestures

Supportive Body Language

- Leaning forward
- Turn face toward partner
- Nodding head vertically (affirmatively)
- Assuming congruent similar body posture
- Maintaining a relaxed/involved body posture
- Tilting head slightly to the side
- Keeping a close and comfortable distance from the partner
- Maintaining an open body posture
- Crossing legs toward partner
- Light physical touching
- Engaging in natural gestures

Silence

Never be afraid of periods of silence. Silence can be a useful tool in negotiation. Some sales training suggests that you state your price and then put duct tape over your mouth because the first person to speak after you have completed your message is the loser. Many people, including possibly your counterpart, are uncomfortable with silence and feel compelled to say something just to fill the empty space—at the risk of saying too much. It is easy to get into trouble by saying the wrong thing or giving away something you ought not to give.

Peter: "The price we are offering is $25,000."

David: "Wow. That's much higher than I was expecting."

[SILENCE]

It is usually at this point that Peter begins to feel uncomfortable and think about how to reduce the price or (worse still) he becomes defensive of his price.

Peter: "Well, you have to realize, the cost of materials has gone up, and the man hours for development are…"

Using silence to draw out your counterpart is a common tactic in Asian cultures. When you face a price objection, your response should be to ask a question rather than defend.

Peter: "What price were you expecting?"

From there you are in a good position to explore the benchmarks of their price expectations and may be able to re-anchor their view. You can progress the price element of the discussion, based on your understanding of their needs, assumptions, and research.

Logistical Considerations

The Meeting Place

The choice of meeting place can play an important role in determining the climate for the negotiation. If you schedule the meeting at your counterparts' office, it allows them to be close to their resources, which might make them feel more comfortable and relaxed. You would naturally allow them to choose the seating arrangements and other logistics.

Think of the concessions you will have already extended by giving them the home court advantage, even if only on a psychological basis. As we mentioned in an earlier chapter, there may be strategic or tactical advantages to selecting the meeting venue or allowing your counterpart to select it. Your overall plan for the negotiation will dictate which approach would be most advantageous to you.

There are times when it is in everyone's best interest to select a neutral venue, such as a hotel meeting room, where both parties can ensure that the venue confers no psychological advantage. If stakes are high and emotions are tense, this could be a way to ease tensions and relax suspicions. On the other hand, a neutral site can be pre-arranged to support your strategy. We will address one aspect of that shortly.

We should remember that, in negotiation, as in other parts of business life, first impressions are extremely important—the aesthetics matter as much to the psychological underpinnings of the meeting as your choice of clothing or facial expression. Sloppy presentation reflects poorly on the presenter. That said, there are professional buyers out there who want the atmosphere of the meeting place to be as unfriendly and uninviting as possible (not something that I would ever recommend). At least one major global retail organization often conducts meetings with sales representatives in a bare-bones warehouse with no heat in the winter (and no air conditioning in the summer). Sellers are forced to wait in a large waiting room until a light flashes to let them know they are next. All competitors in a product group are forced into a cramped cubicle to duke it out in front of one purchasing agent. The psychological ramifications of these powerful nonverbal cues is to make it clear that they are unwanted guests beseeching the global company to hear their pleas. Guess who has the position of power in these meetings?

Table Positioning

This is another important strategic element of a negotiation that most people take for granted. The psychological underpinnings of table placement and seating arrangements (even the size and shape of the tables) can have a profound effect on the outcome of the meeting. I am bewildered that more people don't recognize this, but I appreciate the competitive advantage this knowledge affords me.

The Competitive/Defensive Position

- An appropriate setup for a first business meeting

- Can create a competitive or defensive climate in a business context

- The table becomes a natural barrier between the individuals

- Allows good eye contact

The Cooperative Position

- Creates an opportunity to work jointly with another person

- Allows good eye contact and the opportunity to build rapport

- Invades personal and intimate zones

- A useful setup if you have a long-standing relationship with another person

The Corner Position

- An appropriate setup for a friendly, open conversation

- Allows good eye contact and the use of various gestures

- Easy to observe your counterpart's body language

- The corner of the table can be used as a barrier should you feel threatened or uncomfortable

The Round Table

- The best way to ensure that nobody feels they are disadvantaged by their seating position

- Creates a perception of equality of status and authority

- Creates an informal and more relaxed atmosphere

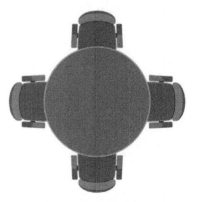

The Art and Science of Persuasion

There is a handful of persuasion techniques top negotiators use to achieve their objectives. Persuasion is just as much science as it is art. I credit researcher and author Dr Robert Cialdini for codifying the science in his fantastic book, "Influence: The Psychology of Persuasion." In this book, he identifies six key agents of influence. When understood and applied correctly, these six principles can vastly aid your negotiation objectives and help you to achieve agreement with your requests.

The Principle of Reciprocity

Reciprocation is a common social norm we have addressed before in this book— we feel obligated to give back to others what they have given to us. As a function of persuasion, always start off with a higher demand so that you allow yourself the opportunity to make a concession toward your counterpart. It will then be more likely that your counterpart will make a concession toward you in return.

It is important to remember that with the rule of reciprocation, we should be acting first, focusing on genuinely enhancing the business prospects of our counterpart. Then he (or she) will be more likely to reciprocate by advancing our business prospects. A practical example of this could be to provide your counterpart with some information that might be really useful to them. When they say, "Thank you," you have your opportunity to register the obligation by saying "you are welcome, I know that you would have done the same for me."

The Principle of Liking

We like people who are like us, and we prefer to do business with people who are like us. We say yes more easily to people we like. Liking is advanced by similarities, cooperative efforts, and compliments.

It is important to focus on the things that are similar between us. While you may be different from your counterpart in ethnicity, religion, or language, you might share values, skills (e.g., you both have been accountants), hobbies, or background (e.g., you have both raised children or worked for the same company).

Liking is also advanced by paying authentic, sincere compliments. Don't you prefer to spend time with people who tell you that you are smart, attractive, or talented?

The Principle of Authority

There is strong pressure in most cultures for compliance with the requests of an authority figure. People want to follow legitimate experts. Demonstrate your credibility and expertise up front by showing your knowledge or experience in a pertinent area. There is no room for bragging or self-aggrandizement. You demonstrate your authority by proof of knowledge, not boasting. If you are not the accepted expert in your field, find established authorities to support your arguments.

You should establish your authority before you engage in negotiations. One of the ways to do this is to become known as a credible counterpart. Counterintuitively, credibility is advanced by owning up to your weaknesses or those of your organization, not by claiming to be the best. Show how your personal background qualifies you to participate in this kind of negotiation. Authority is also easily established by positioning someone else of authority or influence to introduce or recommend you or your services.

The Principle of Scarcity

Fear of losing can be an extremely powerful motivator. Advertisers use it all day every day because it taps into a deep channel of human nature. Items appear more attractive to us if we think we can't have them. You've heard of "playing hard to get."

People want more of what they can get less of and assign more value to opportunities that are less available. In negotiation, we should explain to our counterparts the nature of the elements that are unique to our proposed course of action. A simple way to leverage this principle is to assign deadlines or expiration to your offers.

The Principle of Commitment and Consistency

Once we make a public commitment, we encounter interpersonal pressure to behave consistently with that commitment. People have a strong desire to be (and to appear to be) consistent within their words, beliefs, attitudes, and actions. In negotiation, secure your counterpart's initial commitment and seek to make it public.

The most important commitments are written commitments. This principle is also consistent with what is taught in many sales courses—the notion that you should get many "small yeses" that lead to one "big yes." A practical example of a "small yes" is to ask your counterparts whether they would commit to getting back to you by a certain date and whether they would inform you if their plans change. We live up to what we write down, so secure agreement in writing or by email where possible.

The Principle of Social Proof

People decide what they should do by looking at what others like them do in the same situation. We determine what is correct by finding out what other people think is correct. We should offer references that support our line of argument. It provides us with comfort knowing that we're not the first and/or only people to have made this kind of decision, and it gives our counterpart the security of knowing that others have made the same choice they are considering. An easy example would be to choose a new restaurant to dine in one evening, based on feedback from others.

Cross-cultural Negotiations

There is no denying the fact that the world is getting smaller. The Internet has radically transformed the business world by bypassing borders and linking people in parts of the globe that previously would have never connected. As a result, you are likely to find yourself across the negotiation table from a person who lives on the other side of the planet. Having lived in South Africa, the United Kingdom, and the United States, and having done training and consultancy assignments in nearly 70 countries around the world, I have witnessed the impact first-hand.

This new world of intercultural exchange is both promising and challenging. I strongly encourage you to visit China, India, Africa, and the Middle East, if for no other reason than to experience transacting purchases in the local markets. It's a fascinating study of how business has been done since the dawn of man.

If you find yourself preparing to negotiate with a person or a group from an Asian, Middle Eastern, or African culture, you do yourself no favor by grabbing a book in the airport bookstore on "How To Do Business In China." You might pick up a few pointers that way, but it will be a far cry from the kind of preparation that would truly help you to succeed.

In the weeks leading up to your encounter—indeed, the day you begin your first dialogue with a counterpart from a foreign culture—you should begin asking questions to identify your counterpart's preferences, customs, and expectations. You might find that you possess a view based on stereotypes that have no basis in fact. In some cases, missteps based on racist stereotypes might do you more harm than choosing the wrong word on a document.

In my experience, people in Eastern cultures are usually gracious when a Westerner makes a cross-cultural error, but it is incumbent on all Westerners doing business in an Eastern culture to come prepared with a sensitivity to their customers, especially if the negotiations will take place on their home turf. It shows you to be a professional of high personal development. People want to do business with people who honor them.

If you know that your counterpart will prefer to bow than shake hands (and not just because you saw it in an Asian movie once), then educate yourself on how to bow according to their local culture. There are local norms about how low to bow, what to do with your head, arms, and torso, and so on. Don't assume. Don't be surprised if they lead with a handshake as a sign of honor to you.

In some cultures, particularly Korean and Japanese, copious amounts of alcohol are part of the negotiation process, and it is considered offensive and even suspicious to refuse to get drunk with your counterpart. The background belief is that you are most transparently yourself when you are inebriated. You can pretend to be a good person when you are sober, but when your inhibitions fall down, your true nature appears.

Amusing to me are the differences—subtle as they may be—between American and British culture. Just compare the comedy stylings of British actor John Cleese and American actor Adam Sandler. It is easy to brush these differences under the rug, but if you approach a British executive with an American sales pitch, you will lose him.

I recently showed two very different advertisements to audiences in London and in Texas. One ad had dramatic music, voice-over, and professional-looking stock footage; the other was a montage of testimonies. As I anticipated, the audiences reacted with equal and opposite enthusiasm to the two ads. The British loved the testimonies and were indifferent or put off by the more direct ad copy. The Americans, on the other hand, preferred the dramatic ad style.

Factors Influencing Cross-cultural Negotiations

Negotiating Goal and Basic Concept

How do all counterparts view the negotiation? What cultural filters do they apply to the negotiation itself and to the content being discussed? Is mutual satisfaction the real purpose of the meeting? Do we have to compete? Do they want to win? Different cultures stress different aspects of negotiation. The goal of a negotiation might be a substantive financial outcome or a long-lasting relationship. Know what your counterparts want to achieve and what steps they will find appropriate to achieve it.

Protocol

There are as many kinds of business etiquette as there are nations in the world. Protocol factors that should be considered are dress codes, the number of negotiators, entertainment, degree of formality, gift giving, meeting and greeting, and so on. Again, ask questions starting the first time you interact.

Communication

Verbal and nonverbal communication are key factors for persuasion. The way we express our needs and feelings using body language and tone of voice can determine the way the other side perceives us, and, in fact, positively or negatively contributes to our credibility. Another aspect of communication relevant to negotiation is the direct or indirect approach to exchanging information. Is the meaning of what is said expressed exactly in the words themselves or are there nuances and subtleties? Does "it's impossible" really mean "impossible" or just "difficult to realize?" Always use questions to identify the other side's needs, or assumptions might result in you never finding common interests.

Taking Risks and Avoiding Uncertainty

There is always risk involved in negotiations. The final outcome is unknown when the negotiations commence. The most common dilemma is related to personal relations between counterparts: Should we trust them? Will they trust us? Certain cultures are more risk averse than others—Japan is a good example of caution and risk avoidance. There may be fewer innovative and creative alternatives presented during the negotiation unless there is a strong sense of trust between the counterparts.

View of Time

In some cultures, time is valuable and something to be used wisely. Punctuality and strict adherence to the agenda might be an important aspect of the negotiation, or they might be considered overly formal. In countries such as China or Japan, being late is taken as an insult. In some parts of the United States, the participants might socialize in the lobby for an extra 20 minutes before settling in to review the agenda. Plan investing more time in the negotiating process if you are working in Japan. The main goal when negotiation with an oriental counterpart is to establish a firm relationship, which takes time. Another dimension of time relevant to negotiation is the focus on the past, present, or future. Sometimes the past or the distant future can be seen as part of the present, especially in Latin American countries.

Decision Making Systems

The way members of the other negotiating team reach a decision might give us a hint as to whom we should focus on presenting to. When negotiating with a team, it is crucial to identify the true leader and the person (or group) with the authority to make a decision.

Forms of Agreement

In many cultures, only written agreements stamp a deal. They view it to be the best way to secure everyone's interests in case of any unexpected circumstances. The "deal" might be the contract itself or the relationships between the parties, as in China, where a contract is likely to be in the form of general principles. In this case, if any unexpected circumstances arise, parties prefer to focus on the relationship than the contract to solve the problem.

Power Distance

This refers to the acceptance of authority differences between people. Cultures with low-power distance postulate equality among people, and focus more on earned status than ascribed status. Negotiators from such countries as Great Britain, Germany, and Austria tend to be comfortable with shared authority and democratic structures, When you face high-power distance culture, be prepared for hierarchical structures and clear authority figures.

Personal Style

Our individual attitude toward the other side and biases that we sometimes establish determine our assumptions and can lead the negotiation process toward win-win or win-lose solutions. Do we feel more comfortable using a formal or informal approach to communication? In some cultures, such as the United States, an informal style might help to create friendly relationships and accelerate the problem-solving solution. In China, by contrast, an informal approach is proper only when the relationship is firm and sealed with trust.

One Last Thought On Culture

People change. Cultures change. Norms change. Preferences change. To keep up a thorough discussion of negotiating across cultural differences would require its own book, updated weekly. My point here is not to address all the finer points of distinction between groups, but to demonstrate that your success as a negotiator hinges on your willingness to be sensitive to the differences and adjust your game plan accordingly.

Honoring the nuances between people in our fractalized world is a master key to success in any endeavor, but particularly in negotiation.

Key Takeaways from Chapter Ten

- Mastering the "soft skills" of human interaction—rapport, kindness, honor, personal grooming, and others—is crucial for negotiation success.

- These skills have fallen out of style in many cultures, giving those who still possess them a significant advantage.

- Honor is a master key to success in business. You extend honor to your counterpart by how you conduct yourself during your negotiation and how you engage with them.

- Since research shows that 93% of all communication is nonverbal, mastery of body language—being aware of your own nonverbal messaging and learning to properly read your counterpart's—is vital to correctly navigating a negotiation.

- Preparing the meeting space to foster an environment that supports your strategy and objectives is a best practice for negotiation success.

- There are at least six core principles of persuasion identified by Dr. Robert Cialdini that master negotiators use to move their counterparts toward a favorable outcome.

- When dealing with counterparts from other countries, ethnicities, religions—or even other companies—you must recognize and honor the nuances of the cultures they represent if you are to be successful. A small cultural faux pas can derail a good negotiation.

"Study people more than you study your product or your service and you will be unusually successful."

—Dani Johnson

Apply It To Your Situation

1. Identify three things you learned from this chapter that you want to begin implementing in your negotiations. Highlight the one you want to do first.

   _____

   _____

   _____

   _____

2. Describe how you see the "soft skills" of human interactions operating in your negotiations.

   _____

   _____

   _____

   _____

3. Describe an area of your life where you would like to apply the principles of persuasion more effectively.

   _____

   _____

   _____

   _____

4. What did you learn about negotiation in this chapter that surprised or enlightened you?

   _____

   _____

   _____

   _____

Chapter Eleven: Preparation

Executive Summary

- The difference between professional negotiators and amateurs (or successful and unsuccessful) can be measured in the effectiveness of their preparation.

- Opportunity for greater collaboration beyond the point of negotiation is often hidden in plain sight. The Preparation Checklist forces you to think through questions that can uncover opportunities and threats.

- Each section of the Preparation Checklist addresses one of the 4 Pillars of Negotiation.

- By using a checklist, you can avoid embarrassing gaffes and position yourself as a true professional.

Preparing For Negotiation

I enjoy movies, particularly war movies.

Often, the scenes I enjoy most are the ones where they intercut the two sides preparing for the climactic battle. You see them rolling out maps and blueprints, thinking through their strategic advantages and disadvantages. They design and build weapons to capitalize on their opponents' weaknesses. While movies like *Rocky* and *The Karate Kid* show montages of the hero training for a fight (over inspiring music), it is relatively generic training compared to the detailed battle planning you see in a movie like *Lincoln*.

If you think of your negotiation as a battle, your preparation is where the battle is won or lost.

Missed Opportunities

This is the secret sauce. This is where deals are made and lost.

And this is where I see one of the biggest mistakes in negotiation being made—the mistake of failing to adequately prepare before entering a negotiation. I shudder to think about how many billions (or even trillions) of dollars have been left on negotiation tables around the world because of a failure to engage in meaningful preparation.

I don't know how many times I have heard comments like this: "The big meeting at ABC Company is tomorrow at 10:00. Let's meet at Starbucks in the lobby of their building at 9:30 and write down the things we want to ask for." It would be laughable, but the sad truth is that comments like that almost always lead to failure.

Considering everything we have covered so far in this book, how can you expect to walk into a negotiation unprepared and just "wing it?" Even if you were to accidentally achieve your objectives for the meeting, think of the potential additional opportunity you would have sacrificed because you weren't prepared to look for it.

What You Don't Know Can Keep You Broke

As we review the 4 Pillars of Negotiation, we see several areas where opportunity can hide. If you haven't done your due diligence to understand your counterpart, you will miss them all, along with all the potential benefits they carry:

Vision

- Your counterpart's interests, preferred strategies, and preferred tactics, and how they relate to yours

- Creativity to encourage deal making

- What you know about their values and motivations

Value

- Your counterpart's deal objectives, real base, aspiration base, and how they align or conflict with yours

- Your BATNA and anything you know about your counterpart's BATNA

- Alternatives your counterpart has available

- How you compare to your competitors in your counterparts' eyes

- Concessions you are willing to make

Process

- Team roles and responsibilities
- How you plan to frame the meeting
- Questions you want to ask
- Agenda items
- Meeting venue, logistics and attention to detail

Relationship

- Location and climate of the location
- People directly and indirectly involved in the negotiation
- Cultural considerations
- How should greetings be conducted? Should we make name tags? What is the appropriate body language?
- What forms of persuasive communication should we use?

Can you see some of the places where opportunity could be hiding? You may be aligned with your counterpart on a value that seems unrelated to the topic you are negotiating, but what if there is a different type of partnership hidden in that shared value? There is so much room for additional opportunities, and yet, so many people enter into negotiations with no clear idea of what they want to achieve from the meeting, let alone what they stand to gain by probing just a little further.

The Negotiation Preparation Checklist

Since negotiation is not linear, but complex, it is not useful to think about a step-by-step approach to prepare for a negotiation. It's rather more effective to think in terms of due diligence. In that light, we've prepared a simple checklist that covers all of the possible considerations that might influence a negotiation. Each section corresponds to one of the four Pillars of Negotiation. You can find a digital copy of the checklist when you visit **www.negotiationeurope.com/negotiation-preparation-checklist**. I've also included small thumbnails of the four sections here in the book. [Chad to insert thumbnails]

The Negotiation Preparation Checklist is one of the most powerful negotiation tools I have ever used. In my mind, this is where your competitive edge lies. This is where you win deals you would have lost otherwise. This is where you differentiate yourself from all of your competitors. This is where you create opportunities and synergies you would otherwise have missed. This is where successful negotiators are born.

Section 1—Vision (Yellow)

In summary, this section aligns with our first pillar—Vision.

Checkbox:		PILLAR 1: VISION			
☐	Our Key Interests Identified:	1)			
☐	Counterpart's Key Interests Identified:	1)			
☐	Our Preferred Strategy:	(select from list)		Counterpart's Preferred Strategy	(select from list)
☐	Appropriate Negotiation Tactics:	1)			
☐	Tactics to be Potentially Deployed by Counterpart:	1)			

Why are you entering into a negotiation? What do you hope to gain from it? As obvious as these questions might sound, you would be startled at how many people enter into negotiations without knowing the answers to them. Even professional negotiators sometimes enter the ring with nothing more than a vague assumption about what they need and hope to get.

Goals and outcomes must be measurable. If you don't know exactly where the target is, you can never be sure if you've hit it. Writing down your goals, positions, and interests makes them more concrete and measurable. It also allows you to set them side by side with your counterparts' goals, position, and interests so that you can look for additional opportunities for synergy.

Are you in a position to be competitive or should you plan to be more cooperative? What would you gain by approaching this negotiation more competitively?

Now, turn the table and, based on the information you have, make an educated guess about what strategy your counterpart might assume. What motivates your counterpart similarly to you? How do you look when you view yourself from the other side, especially compared with other options? What tactics have you seen them use before? What does it suggest about their level of assertiveness?

How does this line of thinking help you prepare?

Do you know your counterparts' goals, priorities, and interests? If not, it's ok. This bit of information—actually this lack of information—is instructive to you in that it shows you where you need to do some more research and (maybe more importantly) plan some questions to ask during the negotiation. Frankly, if you are coming to the negotiation table with no clear idea of your counterpart's goals, priorities, values, and interests (stated or unstated), you are in for a rough ride and possibly a short career. By this point, you should know at least this much about your counterpart.

If you have engaged with this counterpart before, you should have a pretty good idea of how they behave during negotiations. Knowing that information, as we stated before, allows you to prepare your approach and keeps you from being caught off-guard or offended. That alone should boost your confidence.

Let's say that, based on previous history and a review of their alternatives, you've determined that they're going to be competitive. Now you don't have to be surprised or taken aback when they come with an extreme offer; your preparation led you to expect it. They will likely lead with a good cop/bad cop tactic, and they might even say, "take it or leave it." Where you might have been offended by those tactics in the past, now you can just respond to the tactic without getting offended. You know it is part of the game. You no longer react emotionally to it; you just follow through with your strategy. Your new, unemotional response can turn the tide for you with this counterpart.

This is why you want to think about these things in advance.

Section 2—Value (Blue)

In many ways, this is the engine room of the negotiation. Here you will identify your objectives for the negotiation and list them out, such as salary, contract terms, or how to split revenue from merchandising and advertising.

Checkbox:		PILLAR 2: VALUE					
☐	Our Prioritised Deal Objectives:	Objective		Real Base	Aspiration Base	Conflicting Objective	Shared Objective
		1)					
		2)					
		3)					
		4)					
☐	Counterpart's Anticipated & Prioritised Deal Objectives:	Objective		Real Base	Aspiration Base	Conflicting Objective	Shared Objective
		1)					
		2)					
		3)					
		4)					
☐	Our BATNA:	1)					
☐	Counterpart's BATNA:	1)					
☐	Concession Strategy: we will trade as follows	1)	for				
		2)	for				
		3)	for				

For each of those objectives, you will pick a Real Base and an Aspiration Base—the minimum level you will accept and then your ideal level (remember, it might not be money). Once you've selected an objective for your side, you also need to enter that objective under your counterpart's list of objectives. This is important because you want to find a Zone of Possible Agreement (ZOPA) where overlaps show us opportunities.

Shared and Conflicting Objectives

You will then mark whether each objective is conflicting or shared. This can help you set up certain conversations and avoid others. In business, what's the number one conflicting objective? Price, right? As a negotiator, should you start with the conflicting objectives or the shared objectives? Start with the shared objectives. Remember, in life what you focus on is what you get.

You might recall that I used this image earlier in the book to demonstrate that we have more in common than in conflict with our counterparts across the table. The wise negotiator identifies and emphasizes the shared objectives before discussing the conflicting objectives.

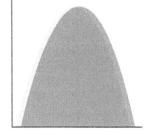

Focus on Shared Objectives

Companies will sometimes ask me, "What do you do when you're in deadlock?" I have one client in particular who often finds themselves in that situation. The mistake they make consistently is that they focus attention on the differences they have with their counterparts. You're never going to solve problems or build relationships by putting the focus on what separates you. The fortune is in what unites you.

There is a Native American story about two wolves who meet every day to fight for dominance of the pack—one represents good and the other represents evil. The one you feed is the one that wins. If you continue to focus on the problems, guess what gets bigger? The problems. You have to bring the focus onto what is good—shared values, priorities, goals, and interests—not on the points of disagreement. The disagreements will obviously come to the surface (after all, solving them is often the point of the negotiation), so you don't have to lead with them. Build a bridge with shared values.

What are some values and priorities almost all businesses have in common? Profitability. Growth. Market share. Quality. Safety. Corporate responsibility. Those are the things you talk about first before you get into topics where there might be conflict. Give special attention to shared values and objectives that have significance for this conversation and build from there.

BATNA

Then you identify the BATNAs—Best Alternative to a Negotiated Agreement. These are your "no deal" options. What are you going to do if there's no deal? That's all BATNA is. In this case, if we can't do X, maybe we have to do Y instead. If we can't come to an agreement with this team, we might have to find another team.

The quality of the alternatives you have available will determine the power balance. Does this information cause you to change which strategy are you going to use? Who should make the first offer and at what level of aspiration? Should you anchor the negotiation or should you let your counterpart anchor it? Answer these questions here.

Concession Strategy

Finally, you have to develop a concession strategy. If making concessions builds satisfaction, then it behooves us to be ready to make some concessions.

Plan the concessions you will make when they push back against your offer. If you know the objection will be over price, you might prepare to respond, "Well, I can take a little bit less, but maybe you can cover the cost of shipping in return?"

Section 3—Process (Green)

This is the operational section of the plan in that it serves as a checklist to make sure we are fully prepared for the meeting.

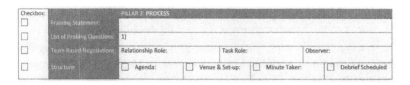

Checkbox:		PILLAR 3: PROCESS						
☐	Framing Statement:							
☐	List of Probing Questions:	1)						
☐	Team Based Negotiations:	Relationship Role:		Task Role:		Observer:		
☐	Structure:	☐ Agenda:	☐ Venue & Set-up:		☐ Minute Taker:		☐ Debrief Scheduled	

Based on the plan we've developed in the yellow and blue sections, we can think through some of the logistics of the meeting. The green section allows us to establish who is on our team and what each person's role will be. Here, we will chart out how we want to frame the meeting, and some probing questions we want to use to fill in the gaps in our information.

This is also where we will confirm that we have written out and confirmed the agenda with the other team, booked and confirmed the meeting space, chosen the layout of the room, and scheduled a debrief for the meeting.

Section 4—Relationship (Red)

Finally, as we move into the red section of this form, we think through the relational aspects of our engagement. In the green section, we identified the logistical side of the venue and setup; here we think about the climate of that space. How are we going to greet the other party when they arrive? Do we want to make them feel welcome or intimidated? Do we want to create a comfortable space? What kind of body language do we want to use to reinforce our messages?

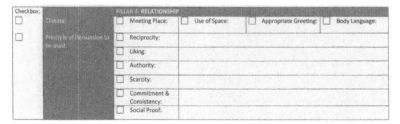

Checkbox:		PILLAR 4: RELATIONSHIP			
☐	Climate:	☐ Meeting Place:	☐ Use of Space:	☐ Appropriate Greeting:	☐ Body Language:
☐	Principle of Persuasion to be used:	☐ Reciprocity:			
		☐ Liking:			
		☐ Authority:			
		☐ Scarcity:			
		☐ Commitment & Consistency:			
		☐ Social Proof:			

Finally, we will choose the persuasive styles we will use to make our case.

Your Strategic and Tactical Advantage

Pilots use checklists before every single flight, to ensure that all of the equipment works as designed. Smart pilots know that just because a piece of equipment worked the last time they flew doesn't guarantee it will work this time. Even the smallest failure can cause a deadly plane crash, so even if they have run the checklist thousands of times, they go through every step as if it were the first time.

Negotiation might not be a life-or-death scenario like a plane crash (although there are times when it is), but whether you are negotiating a billion-dollar deal, national sovereignty, or a simple home lease, eighty percent of the success of your negotiation lies in your preparation.

By walking through this preparation process, you not only avoid embarrassing gaffes and missteps, you align your approach with best practices that consistently lead to success. You position yourself and your team as well-prepared professionals. In all likelihood, unless your counterpart has read this book, they will not be as well-prepared for the negotiation and they will leave the room wondering how you did it.

Key Takeaways from Chapter Eleven

- Preparation is everything. It can be the source of your confidence, your competitive advantage, the confirmation of what you know and don't know, and your treasure map to uncovering opportunities you would otherwise have missed.

- Opportunity is hiding in all four pillars of negotiation, if you are willing to look for it.

- The Negotiation Preparation Checklist is like a pilot's tool in that it allows you to confirm that you have thought through every aspect of the negotiation meeting.

> *"Unfortunately, there seems to be far more opportunity out there than ability... We should remember that good fortune often happens when opportunity meets with preparation."*

> —Thomas Edison

Apply It To Your Situation

1. Describe how your preparations have looked prior to reading this chapter.

   _____

   _____

   _____

   _____

2. Describe how the Preparation Checklist could simplify your work.

   _____

   _____

   _____

   _____

3. What did you learn about negotiation in this chapter that surprised or enlightened you?

   _____

   _____

   _____

   _____

Chapter 12: Concluding Thoughts

It's fair to say that this book is like a photograph, in that it encapsulates where I stand at this moment in time. It shows what I currently understand about negotiation, and I hope that tomorrow I will understand it more perfectly. As my knowledge grows, I will pass it along to you. May we all put ourselves on paths of continuous growth and development.

Just as we discussed the importance of nonverbal communications throughout this book, you will never gain as much from reading about negotiation as you will in a negotiation training environment, where you are immersed in the practical application of this material. Several times in the development of this book I found myself hampered by the limits of the English language, wishing I could demonstrate the concepts to you in a more tangible way. Perhaps it is because I am more accustomed to presenting these materials in the context of a live training seminar. There is something rich and fulfilling about seeing, hearing, and practicing the skills in a room full of people. Even the best book can never capture that fully, but we have endeavored to distill the essence of the content in a useful way.

That said, let's treat this book as a spring board to greater revelation of the power of negotiation—an invitation to dive in more deeply. If this book has awakened an interest—or at least a curiosity—in negotiation, I invite you to satisfy that interest by attending one of our live training seminars held throughout the year in the United States, Europe, and around the world.

For years, I only offered this training to Fortune 500 clients, but I have come to see that these skills can change other peoples' lives as well: small business owners, professionals, team managers, investors, real estate agents, teachers, government employees, healthcare providers, parents, neighbors, and on and on. In short, everyone can benefit from learning the skills of negotiating with others. If you gained from this book nothing more than a more deeper understanding of your own personality and interpersonal tendencies, I consider that a win for both of us.

I would prize the opportunity to visit with you in person and answer your questions at one of our live training events.

I look forward to meeting you soon.

Made in the USA
Middletown, DE
15 February 2021